JESUS O[N]
Healing Stories

Andre Papineau

Resource Publications, Inc.
160 E. Virginia St., #290
San Jose, CA 95112-5848

Editorial director: Kenneth Guentert
Production editor: Elizabeth J. Asborno
Cover design: Ron Niewald
Cover illustration and production: Andrew Wong
Inside illustrations: Sister Karlyn A. Cauley, SDS

Library of Congress Cataloging in Publication Data
    Papineau, Andre, 1937-
        Jesus on the mend : healing stories for ordinary people / by Andre Papineau.
            p. m.
    ISBN 0-89390-140-7
        1. Healing in the Bible. 2. Bible. N.T. Gospels—Criticism, interpretation, etc. 3. Jesus Christ—Miracles. 4. Bible stories, English—N.T. Gospels. I. Title.
    BS2555.2P274 1989   88-35660
    23.9'55—DC19

5 4 3 2
93 92 91 90

My deepest gratitude to Dan Pekarske, SDS, for his encouragement and the innumerable hours he has spent reviewing and editing the material. Without his help, I would not have written any books. I dedicate this book, then, to Dan: friend, adviser, and fellow Salvatorian.

CONTENTS

INTRODUCTION vii

CHAPTER ONE
Acknowledging the Need

NONSTOP 3
SURVIVOR 11
THEY 19

CHAPTER TWO
Reaching Out For Help

DEMONS 29
INSTALLMENTS 37
OVERRIPE 45

CHAPTER THREE
The Healer's Credentials

TRAVELING STICK 55
THE NAG 63
POWER 73

CHAPTER FOUR
The Healer's Therapy

THE GIFT 81
TOUCH 89
NOTICING 97
CHUTZPAH 105
THANK YOU 113
FEET 121
DREAMER 129
RAGE 137
DAY OFF 145

INDEX 151

INTRODUCTION

If there is one thing all human beings share in common, it is brokenness. We are a broken people. We speak about being all broken up and about having breakdowns that result from being broken up. Sometimes we are bruised, battered, and beaten. Our brokenness is variously described as alienation, estrangement, sin. Brokenness is then conceived of as being broken off or broken apart from others, ourselves, the world, and God. Brokenness is experienced as hurt, and sometimes that hurt is so unbearable that we would prefer death.

There are so many kinds of brokenness that it would take more than the short space here to even list them. To name a few, however, there is the brokenness between husbands and wives, between parents and their children, and between friends. There is brokenness even between a person's body and mind, as well as between nations, racial groupings, and religious traditions. The list could go on and on.

What is needed to mend our brokenness is healing, but not just any kind of healing. For some attempts to heal may themselves cause even worse injury than the original breaking down. They can be demeaning and destructive, as some of the stories to come will illustrate. But there is another kind of healing described in these stories and in the reflections that follow them: a genuine healing that we all need and that all of us are called to bring to one another and to ourselves.

The common thread running through all the following stories is that everybody can be a healer. No one can claim exemption because they lack professional skills or because they may feel too old or too young, etc. The task of healing is not reserved to some special group with advanced training. On the contrary, healing only requires that we be human and that we strive to share that humanity fully and honestly with one another.

It is unfortunate that we tend to identify healing exclusively with the professional caregivers or with faith healers. In so doing our world has become more broken now than it was before the advent of "the professionals." This is not only because now there simply aren't enough professional healers to meet the needs of all who are broken, but also because the kind of healing I am speaking about many of the professionals may know very little about. It is only when all of us rightfully assume our responsibilities to heal that the brokenness so pervasive in our society will be on the mend.

The following stories are imaginative reflections on Jesus' healing miracles. It is best to read the pertinent scriptural passage cited first since it is the frame or context for the story that follows. By their nature the stories are rich and open to many equally valid responses. The reflections are provided to stimulate further consideration about the meaning of the healing presented in each story and are not intended to limit the readers' own creative interpretations and applications. However, the placement of the stories in four chapters has been done to facilitate an understanding of four factors that seem to be at work in the healing experience.

The stories in chapter one, "Acknowledging The Need," illustrate the prerequisite for healing: the admission of one's brokenness. Unless a person can acknowledge his woundedness at least to himself, no healing can take place. Jesus spoke about people who weren't in need of a physician because they didn't acknowledge the need. It is possible to ignore or deny pain for years before finally saying, "I'm in trouble. I need help."

While an acknowledgment of brokenness is a step in the right direction, it isn't enough. A person has to want to be healed. People can know how needy they are without reaching out to get help. Chapter two, "Reaching Out For Help," presents stories that show the necessity for the desire to be healed.

And what about the healer? What enhances and what inhibits the healer's effectiveness? What are the qualifications for being a healer? The healer's credentials are embodied in the stories in chapter three, "The Healer's Credentials."

Finally, the healing process itself is illustrated in the stories in chapter four, "The Healer's Therapy." Most of the stories are contained in this chapter and all of them bring home over and over the same basic points. However, the variety of stories gives the reader an appreciation of these points in strikingly different ways.

Of course many of the stories could be placed in more than one chapter of the book since they easily illustrate more than one factor. But assigning a story to a particular section in the book helps us to focus more clearly on one factor at a time in the healing process. If placing stories in different chapters, as we have done, clarifies what transpires in our own healing activity, then our decision is justified.

CHAPTER ONE
Acknowledging the Need

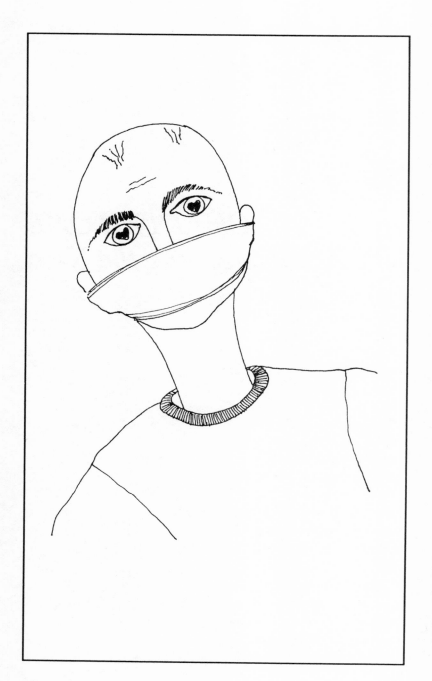

NONSTOP

Mk 7:31-37: Some people brought him a deaf man who had a
speech impediment and begged him to lay his hand on him.

He hadn't always been deaf. Certainly he hadn't always been mute. His friends didn't think what had happened to Mo was funny. Still, they simply couldn't help smiling when they compared the way Mo was before and after his stroke. Mo had been the kind of person who didn't know what the word "listening" meant because he spent all his time talking. He talked nonstop. If he stopped to ask "What?" it was simply to catch his breath, never to find out what someone else had to say.

Morning, noon, and evening he had the first, the last, and the only word in the house. He would ask a question, "What are you going to do today?" and he would immediately answer, "Whatever you do, bundle up because it is cold out there." Or, "How are you doing in school?" and continue, "Let me tell you about my school days." As a result, he never came to know his own family.

When none of them asked a question, Mo made one up just so he'd be able to keep talking. "I can tell by the look on your face—you're wondering why I dunk bagels in my coffee." Then he'd go on for ten minutes answering the question no one dreamed of asking in the first place. "So, you would like to know the difference between a Jericho horse and a Jerusalem horse. Well, let me tell you," or, "It's funny you should be puzzling about the number of outhouses on the highway between Jerusalem and Cairo. I think I can help you. You see..."

It didn't matter if his wife shook her head indicating those weren't her questions. Nor did it matter if his kids were intentionally rude and left the room when he began to answer questions they hadn't asked. He seemed oblivious to all their comings and goings. In other words, for Mo, "nonstop" meant whether his family was there to listen or not.

He was the same way with his friends. But they got more aggressive with his inability to listen and his chronic need to talk. They'd get up and leave the room whenever he spoke for more than two minutes at a stretch. One of the friends would give Mo a time-out sign when his two minutes were up, but Mo never noticed and would drone on. His friends even tried shock tactics. "Mo, we just got word that your house is burning down." But Mo would just convert what they had said into another question, "So, you're interested in knowing how I should feel in a burning house? Well let me tell you..."

Sometimes, during these monologues, they would all get up together and leave the house. Without missing a beat, Mo would follow them outside. Then his friends would rush back and lock the door behind them. Mo was so busy talking that he'd simply stroll over to the window and keep on talking to them from outside.

Finally, everybody just gave up trying to change him.

Then it happened! Mo had a stroke and lost the use of his voice and his hearing. Well, no one was really certain about the hearing loss. Not being able to listen and not being able to hear are so much alike. So people weren't really sure.

4

Mo's loss of speech had social implications that no one had anticipated. His depression was understandable. But he was so conditioned to talk all the time that he continued to move his mouth even though the words didn't come. His friends tried to console him by pointing out that if nothing else, he was getting some facial exercise.

Not only did Mo's speech loss affect him; it affected others as well. For a long time there was a lot of silence at home. No one knew what to say since they had all stopped saying much of anything while Mo had done all the talking. His family would sit around the dinner table, open their mouths and then close them without saying a word because that had been their pattern for years. His friends, on the other hand, were at a loss as to what to do when they got together. They had spent so much of their time thinking of ways to keep Mo quiet that now, with him mute, they had nothing to do.

But Mo was changing gradually. Now that he was forced to be quiet, he began to notice things he had never noticed when he could talk. He noticed when his children were sad or lonely. He picked up his wife's anxieties. When he was with friends, he began to pay attention to how their faces and their bodies registered fear or hate or anger. Mo saw the slightest moisture forming in their eyes as they related some moving incident. He even began to notice them smiling at him. He felt the warmth of their bodies when they embraced him or patted him on the back. His face responded so openly to his friends' stories about themselves, stories he had never listened to before and now heard for the first time. It wasn't that he actually heard them with his ears. No, he listened to them with his heart. And the eloquence of his eyes spoke so much more gracefully than anything he had ever said with his mouth.

Mo grew to know his family and friends, and they him, for the first time. And for the first time everyone learned to care deeply for him. What could they do to help him, they wondered? They determined to keep their eyes and ears open about what they might do for Mo.

One day one of his friends hurriedly gathered the others. "Jesus is coming to town. You've heard of Jesus, the miracle worker? Let's take Mo to him. It can't hurt and it may be our best and only chance to do something for Mo." They all agreed it was worth a try. So the next day they signaled to Mo what they wanted to do, and with his approval they took him to Jesus.

As usual, there was a great crowd, but Mo's friends managed to get close enough to Jesus to ask him, "Rabbi, we would be deeply grateful if you could help our friend who cannot hear or speak."

Jesus looked over at Mo and smiled. Mo smiled back. There were no words for the next minute but the two men seemed to be on the same wave length to which no one else had access. Then Jesus spoke to Mo's friends. "Let him come with me for a while." And to those around him, Jesus said, "I'll be back shortly." Then he led Mo by the arm to a quiet spot about a three-minute walk away.

Jesus looked at Mo and put his fingers in Mo's ears. Massaging them gently, he then removed one finger, moistened it with saliva, and then motioned Mo to open his mouth. Jesus touched the tongue with his moistened finger, gazing all the while into Mo's eyes. Finally, tears forming in his own eyes, Jesus returned his finger to Mo's ear and lifting his eyes to heaven, he groaned softly. Over and over, "Be opened, be opened, be opened!" Mo heard a popping sound in his ears, and when he opened his mouth to say, "I can hear! I can hear!" he actually heard himself speak. He was overcome! He shouted, "I can talk! I can talk! There are so many things I have to say. I can hardly wait to get back and tell my friends. They must be dying to hear my voice again!"

When he finally slowed down for a gulp of breath, he noticed that Jesus was still gazing steadily at him and still murmuring over and over, "Be opened, be opened."

"But I can hear, I can hear. And I can talk again too. You've healed me. I'm 100 per cent! Can't you tell? I'm back like I was!" Mo's torrent of words dried up as if someone had turned off a faucet. And in his silence he heard over and over, "Be opened, be opened." Mo realized that Jesus didn't want Mo back like he had been. And Mo didn't want that either.

"Now I understand," he said quietly, and after a long pause, "What good is hearing without listening or speaking without ever really talking with someone? Old habits die hard," he said sheepishly and studied the ground.

Jesus too had become silent. He reached out and gently raised Mo's head until their eyes met. The two were smiling through their tears. "Let's go," Jesus said, "your friends will be anxious to talk with you."

Reflection: Do You Know What I Mean?

A number of years ago an elderly woman went to one of the college campuses and set up a little tent. She put a sign on the front flap that read: I Will Listen To All Your Problems For A Nickel. It wasn't long before there was a long line of college students in front of her tent. One by one students would go in, sit down, tell her all their problems, and then leave the tent. They all remarked what a good listener she was, and added that she was very understanding. What they didn't know was that the woman was deaf!

And perhaps it didn't matter. It certainly works to Mo's advantage to lose his hearing because when he can no longer hear he begins to listen as he never listened before. Just as the elderly woman had an understanding heart, so too Mo begins to listen with his heart. And that is a gift that proves to be of greater worth than his hearing.

Interestingly, Mo's healing begins to take place once he loses his hearing and his speech. Only then does he really begin to notice what is going on around him. The healing is not complete, however, until he goes to Jesus to be cured of his affliction. Yet, even after he receives his hearing and his speech back, he still needs to be opened. "Be opened. Be opened." Jesus knows that openness is a total response of the person, not merely the elimination of a physical handicap.

Finally, Mo realizes what Jesus wants of him. It is then that Mo is not only completely healed but he himself becomes the healer. Anyone who grows in awareness of his inability to listen is in the process of self healing. Opening ourselves to our fears, anxieties, and insecurities, we listen as we have never listened before. In being heard, that dimension of the self is being healed by another dimension that heals. We learn to listen to ourselves, and this inner dialogue is a dialogue or exchange in which the healer and the healed come into being. Healing on the "intrapersonal" level is essential if we are to experience the healing on the "interpersonal" level. Listening to ourselves and listening to others go hand in hand.

Just how important is it that we listen to one another? An expression we use over and over during the day is "Do you know what I mean?" We speak a few words and then we interject, "Do you know what I mean?" Sometimes we just say "Know what I mean?" or "D'ya know?" In using this expression we are not asking for a formal analysis of our statement. No, we are looking for comprehension of our total meaning as persons. We want to know if we mean anything. It is an isolating experience not to be understood at all or to be met with a blank stare or an uncomprehending silence. When we hear a sincere "I know what you mean," then we know what we mean to ourselves as well as to the other. We are liberated from the isolation of not only being not understood by others but also of not making any sense to ourselves. I have an appreciation of my own meaning (that is, who I am and what I am about in life) if there is another who can receive my meaning and help me clarify for myself what may not be all that clear.

Healing in this story is in listening, and it too is the kind of healing that is possible for all persons who are able to admit their need for this healing. The admission itself is the first step in healing and being healed.

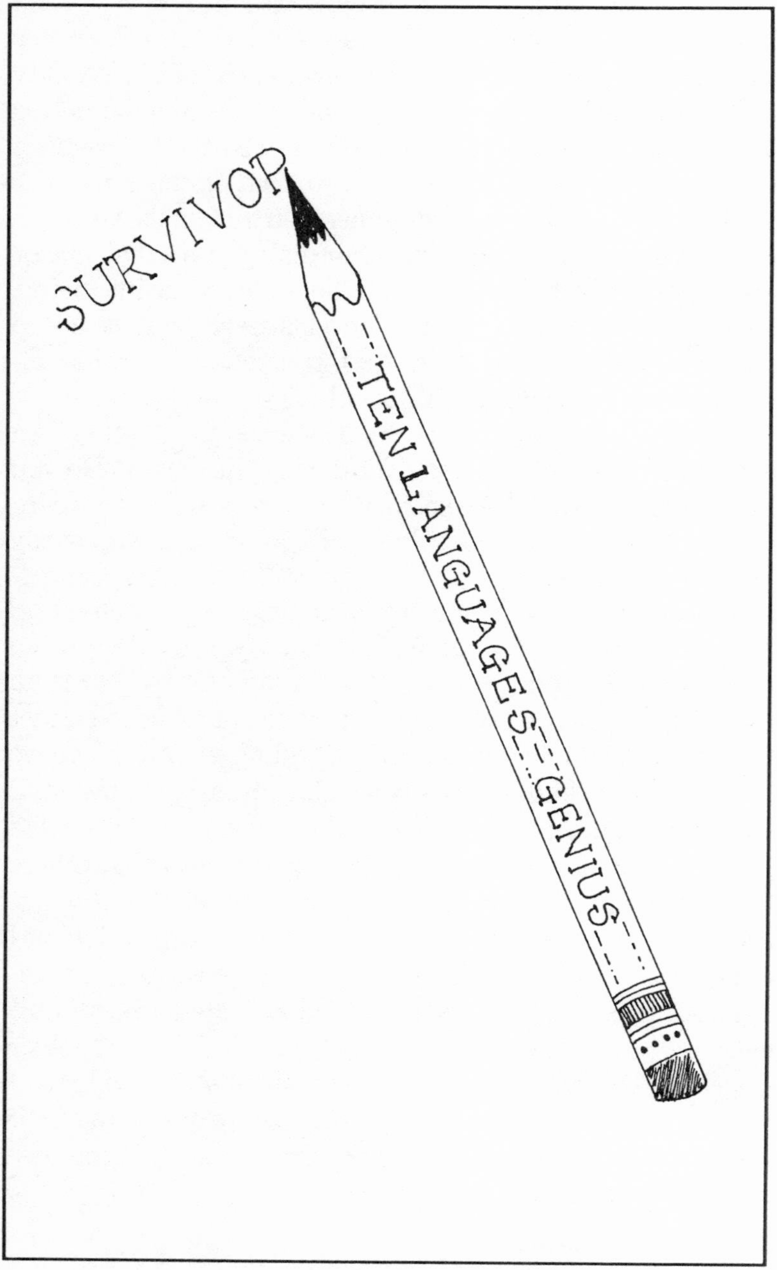
SURVIVOR
TEN LANGUAGES GENIUS

SURVIVOR

Mk 10:46-52: Jesus asked him, "What do you want me to do for
you?" "Rabboni," the blind man said, "I want to see."

Bartimaeus was a survivor. He may have been blind, but he
was feisty. He had to be. He had grown streetwise and
knew just how to work the crowds. When he first started, he had
just looked for pity. Wearing an "I am blind" sign on his back, he
stood passively in the middle of the sidewalk waiting for people
to drop a coin or two in his cup. But something inside him said
that while even though he was blind, he didn't have to live out
his days standing in the middle of a sidewalk with a tin cup in his
hand. He decided then and there he wouldn't let his blindness
stop him from living like everybody else.

So, it wasn't long before he started selling pencils first, then
erasers, and finally canes that glowed in the dark. And he
didn't just sell them. No, he hawked them. "These incredible
pencils can write in every known language," he would tell
potential customers. Then, he'd haul out his erasers and tell
them, "And these erasers can erase anything written in any
known language and then some." And the canes? With a
smile on his face, he'd croon, "Oh, these canes glow in the
dark; they're made especially for people who can't see and
want to see where they're going."

Bart had quite a flair for selling pencils, erasers, and canes. He always buttered up a potential customer. He'd only need to hear the voice of his potential customer and the flattery started up. To a young man he would say, "You, son of David, here is an eraser to wipe out all the Goliath's in your life." To another man, "David's son, do yourself a favor and imitate your father- of-old's other son, Solomon the Wise. Buy the pencil that writes all the words of wisdom." To yet another, "Adam, have you been searching for your son, Cain, lately? Here he is ready to walk hand in hand with you." To yet another, "You with the beard of Moses, here is the cane to create a path through any sea of people." Of course, everyone was usually delighted with Bart's pitch and more often than not ended up buying a pencil or an eraser or a cane.

Sometimes, someone would come along, hear the pitch and tell Bart, "If you saw me or knew me you wouldn't call me a David or a Solomon or a Moses."

But Bart would reply, "Who cares what you look like or how smart you are—you've got the voice of a Moses. You've got the sound of David. Ooh, such a commanding voice you have." And Bart sounded so convincing that often people who were feeling terribly low would come by just to hear Bart tell them how great they sounded. It wasn't unusual on occasions like that for Bart to get rid of five pencils at a time. That always made his day. For on the one hand, he was able to lift someone else's spirits if just for a couple of minutes, while on the other hand, he could pocket a few extra cents. He'd be so delighted with what he had done that he'd say to himself, "Who needs to see? I can get along quite well the way I am, thank you."

Of course, Bart had difficult days too. There were always street bullies to contend with. They would push him down, rough him up, and run off with the few cents he had made during the course of the day. Bart would pick himself up and shake his fists at the assailants he couldn't see. "Why, if I could only see, I'd punch..." but then he'd catch himself and mutter, "Who needs to see? I can manage quite well the way I am, thank you."

Incidents like these didn't stop Bart from working the crowds, however. He always managed to produce another box of pencils or erasers and he always had a cane or two hidden somewhere for just such emergencies.

Bart always moved to where he thought the traffic would be heaviest. Wherever there were crowds, he would be. If he thought some dignitary would be in a particular part of town, then Bart would talk someone into leading him there by the hand. He'd apologize for having to ask the person to take time out to help him. "If I could see, there wouldn't be any need for you..." but Bart would then go silent. He didn't want to dwell on what was an impossibility as far as he was concerned. Once at his destination, he would begin advertising by calling out as loudly as he could, sometimes to the annoyance of the crowd. It was his only way of drawing their attention, however, and even if it meant drawing their anger, he hoped they would buy something even if it was just to silence him.

One day, Bart found out from one of his customers that Jesus, a popular rabbi, would be in the neighborhood for lunch. He had heard of Jesus and admired what he had heard. The thought entered his mind that maybe Jesus could help him see. "Perhaps Jesus..." but then he dismissed the thought. "Forget it! I wouldn't bother wasting his time." For the moment, he was delighted that Jesus would be working the crowds in Bart's own neighborhood because that meant Bart's business was sure to pick up. With an extra supply of pencils and erasers, just to make sure that he had enough to sell, Bart stationed himself on the nearest curb before the crowd arrived.

In a matter of minutes he could hear the people moving in his direction, signaling that Jesus had arrived. With the instinct of a survivor, he launched into his spiel shouting, "Pencils! Erasers! Canes! Pencils! Erasers! Canes!" And then as though the next words were part of the sales pitch, "Jesus, son of David, have mercy on me!" Bart himself was startled that he had altered his sales pitch to include this expression. "Pens! Write in ten languages! Erasers! Erase in ten languages! Canes that glow in the dark! Jesus have mercy on me!" Well, just as he expected, the crowd said, "Shut up! Keep quiet! You know where you can put your pencils and erasers not to mention your canes!"

But this delighted Bart. "At least I know they hear me!" So, even at the risk of getting a beating with his own canes he shouted all the louder, "Pencils! Write in ten languages! Erasers! Erase in ten languages! Canes that glow in the dark! Jesus, son of David, have mercy on me!" But now something happened. He began to hear his own voice as if he were the only one around. Had the crowd gone? No, he could just make out the people around him whispering "Shhhh" to one another. Then from all around him he heard quiet voices urging him to get up and go to Jesus—that he had nothing to fear! Bart was getting more than he had bargained for. He had wanted attention, yes, but not the center of attention.

"Get up! Jesus is waiting. You called him! Now, go to him!" the voices around him continued. Hands began nudging him forward. Bart inched along almost involuntarily. He didn't know where he was going or exactly why either. But he felt as if he were being drawn forward by some magnetic force. All the while Bart kept mumbling quietly, "Pencils. Erasers. Canes. Mercy, have mercy!" When finally he felt a hand stop him, he said with the instinct of a survivor, "Son of David, would you like to buy a pencil? It writes in ten different languages." All he heard was a gentle laugh and Bart's reaction was what it had always been. "You have a nice laugh and a nice voice, like David's own son." But this time he really meant it.

Then Bart heard the voice of David's own son ask, "What can I do for you?"

Bart was going to say, "How about taking five pencils and erasers off my hands!" but instead he blurted out words he never thought he would hear himself saying, "I want to see!" The words had the sound of a man who had learned to fight up until this point in life and wasn't about ready to stop now. His voice was firm but not arrogant. And as soon as he had cried out the word "see," he felt a sharp pain in his eyes. Gradually, he became accustomed to the light that dispelled the darkness of years. Blinking repeatedly, he could make out the figure in front of him touching him with both hands on his shoulders. "Your faith has healed you," Jesus said.

Bart hadn't yet grasped what had happened. He still continued to mutter, "Pencils. Erasers. Canes." But when he came to the words, "Jesus have mercy on me," his eyes welled up with tears as he now followed the man up the road, the man who had the voice of the Son of David.

Reflection:
Lust For Life

Survivors are believers; and what they believe in is their own abilities to stay alive. That is no small accomplishment for those who have been beaten and battered, both literally and figuratively, all of their lives. Black slaves on plantations and Jews in concentration camps are among the most obvious examples of people struggling to survive oppression. But anyone who has suffered discrimination because of creed, color, or sex and not given up without a fight is also a survivor.

Some survive not only the oppression of others, but also what nature has done to them. Children with diseases that leave them blind or lame or otherwise handicapped as well as whole communities suffering human and material loss from tornadoes, floods, fires, etc., are also survivors when they refuse to dwell on their losses or lie on their backs in despair.

Bart is a survivor because he believes in his abilities to stay alive. Not only does he have to struggle against his blindness, he also has to struggle to meet his bodily needs and protect himself from physical abuse. To say he believes in his abilities is to say he relies on a combination of an instinctive desire to live, a resilient spirit, and just plain gutsiness. He is not ready to go out with a whimper, and he's certainly not ready to cash in before his time. However, the self-reliance that serves Bart so well also creates a problem for him, the kind of problem many of life's survivors face.

Self-reliance can become excessive, making it difficult for the survivor to admit any need for others. Bart's like that. As a result the healing he needs is not only from his blindness, but from his chronic need to go it alone. Because survivors frequently make it on their own for so long, some may consider it a real weakness to own their unrecognized longing to rely on others for help. Consequently, a deep conflict is generated.

However, in time, Bart's desire for healing is greater than his resistance to asking for help. He blurts out to Jesus that he wants to see but not before hesitating and considering retreating to the sales pitch, an expression of his independence. The survivor in Bart doesn't easily give up the defensive posture because it was developed to protect a self painfully assaulted in so many different ways over the years. Understandable as this is, until he is able to lower that defense, healing cannot take place.

None of us may be survivors to the same extent as Bart or the other survivors described here. But it is more than likely that we have been hurt in some area of our lives and that, like Bart, we have learned to defend ourselves from further pain by being gutsy and independent. Healing for us, as for Bart, comes in recognizing and lowering our defensive posture so we can at last cry out our own need to be healed.

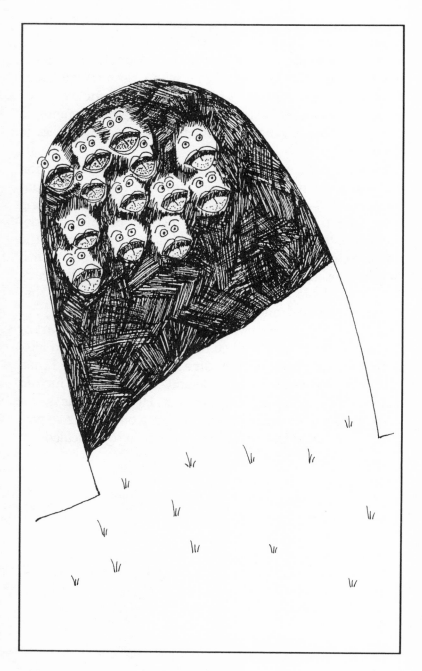

THEY

Mark 1:21-28: All who looked on were amazed. They began to ask one another: "What does this mean? A completely new teaching in a spirit of authority! He gives orders to unclean spirits and they obey!"

No one knew who he was when he walked down the streets past their homes. No doubt they ought to have known him since he had been walking down those same streets for several years now. What may seem surprising is that they did go out of their way to try to know him but to no avail. All they discovered was the power of some alien force that held sway over him, and it was this power that kept people at a distance. And what was this power? Well, you would gradually discover it if you stopped him on the street and asked him certain questions.

For example, if you asked him what he thought, he wouldn't be able to say. If you asked what he felt about something, he wouldn't be able to tell you. Finally, if you asked him what he would choose to do about a particular issue, he wouldn't know what to answer. Simple questions, surely: What do you think? How do you feel? What would you do? Oh, he could have told you what Rabbi Feldstein thought, or how Ms. Goldblatz felt, or what the Torah prescribed as interpreted by the commentaries. But what he could not do was tell you what he thought.

"What is it like outside—is it nice?"

"Well, they tell me it is nice, so I suppose it is."

"And what did you feel about the new play at the Jerusalem Hilton? Did you like it?"

"The review in the *Jerusalem Times* is positive about it—they say the play is heartwarming."

"And what would you do if your daughter got pregnant?"

"I would ask a counselor or my mother what to do."

Whoever this man was, he could answer your question about who thought what, who felt what, and who would do what. He just couldn't tell you what he thought or felt or would do on anything. Why? Not because he didn't want to tell you but because he had never permitted himself to think or feel or do anything on his own.

"What do you think?"

"I don't know."

"What do you feel? Do you feel?"

"I don't know."

And it wasn't that he just didn't want to tell you how he'd act in a particular situation—no, he really didn't know what he'd do because he never permitted himself to agonize over what he might do.

Many people were curious as to why he couldn't answer these questions when they were put to him. It was safe to be this way, very safe. Whoever he was, he couldn't go wrong.

"What do you think about divorce? What are your feelings? Where do you stand?"

"Well, the rabbi says..."

"And what do you feel about the homeless?"

"Well others tell me..."

"But what do you feel—not the church, not the synagogue, not your political party, not your friends, not your neighbors, or your wife—what do you feel?"

And the answer would always be, "Well, they..." and of course he would be delivered from considering what he felt. He was safe from himself only to find his soul safely in "their" hands. For if you do not think or feel or act, but "they" think for you, feel for you, do for you what you will not do—then where is the "you" in you? What has happened to you? You are not there. You have been taken over and all that remains is the grin of the Cheshire cat that is "they."

People wondered if there was any chance of the man ever changing. But there had to be a "who" inside to feel the oppressive weight of what "they" thought or felt or did in him. There had to be a "who" to feel the pain of being buried alive, of being possessed, and to struggle to be free to assume responsibility for his own life. And besides all this, one thing more was required for the man to change.

He needed the example of one who thought his own thoughts, felt his own feelings, did what he thought he must do. Such a figure would be threatening, very threatening to one who had not thought, felt, or done anything on his own for so long. Such a figure would challenge him to assume responsibility for his own life—to forgo the safety of what "they" thought, felt, and did in him. Yet, at the same time, the thought of being in the presence of such a person was also appealing. It offered the possibility of liberation from the increasingly oppressive "they."

What finally happened to the man? There appeared in the local synagogue a man by the name of Jesus, a man who taught with authority. He was a man who authored what he said, that is, he wrote the script for his own life. He was not afraid to proclaim what he thought and felt about life. Everybody in the synagogue was amazed because Jesus didn't teach as the scribes did— parroting what others thought or felt or would do. He was clearly his own person.

Among those in the synagogue that day was the man possessed by "they." He had heard of Jesus and at first was drawn to him because here was one more teacher whose opinion he could use and add to "they." Yet, as the man sat listening to Jesus he became more and more agitated. Obviously Jesus was not a man who lived by "they" and this threatened him. Nonetheless, he felt attracted to Jesus because he began to recognize that this person was free from the voices that controlled his own life.

What should he do? What did Jesus want? Why didn't Jesus just come out and tell him plainly what to do? He tried to rise and leave but could not find the strength. He tried to approach Jesus, but it was as if "they" held him back. Then on the verge of tears he found himself shouting, "Jesus, what do you want of us? Have you come to destroy us?" With the little strength that was left in him, he lunged toward Jesus' feet and lay there moaning, "Jesus, what do you want of us? Have you come to destroy us?"

Jesus knelt down and put his hands gently on the man's shoulders and said, "Be quiet! Come out of the man!"

"No, we cannot leave! He needs us! He is nothing without us!" The voices were defiant.

The man moaned again but this time it was his voice, not theirs that cried out, "Save me! I don't want them. I don't need them anymore. I, I," he struggled, "I am!" No sooner had he shouted "I am" than a quiet came over him, tears rolled gently down his cheeks, and he got up off the floor with Jesus' help.

"How do you feel?" Jesus asked.

"They say..." the man started out, then checked himself, "I feel fine."

"And what will you do with your new life?" Jesus was curious not only about the details of the man's future but more basically whether the man saw himself as having a future of his own at all.

"I'm going to ask Rabbi..." Again he caught himself, smiled and went on, "I'm going to take time to go off by myself to decide that. But I'll decide."

"Good," Jesus said approvingly. "But keep an eye out for 'them' because 'they' want to come back. They are always lurking in the shadows, waiting." Then Jesus put his arm around the man and they walked out of the synagogue together—just the two of them.

Reflection: Who's There?

What is the price we pay in relying excessively on what others think, feel, and do in order to live our lives? The loss of a sense of self, of our integrity, of authenticity. The subjective experience of that loss is depression. Or the price we pay may be the failure to achieve any sense of self at all. Once more depression may be the felt experience of such a failure; and whether loss or failure is the price, the weight of depression is a very heavy burden to bear.

It is difficult to imagine how many people in our society are depressed or depression-prone because of their excessive need to do or think or feel according to what they believe others expect. Many children miss out on childhood because they feel they must act like adults to gain their parents' acceptance. Married men and women frequently behave in ways they think their spouses want them to rather than in ways they consider personally satisfying. Many women were brought up to not be too competitive, according to "their" belief that men won't want a wife who has achieved more than they. On the other hand, men are often made to feel that achieving and getting ahead are far more important than developing any relational skills. In all these instances the needs of the self are bypassed in favor of what "they" deem appropriate. The result of pressures not to be the kind of person that one is called to be is the buildup of another pressure: depression, the pressure on the soul.

But the pressure of depression is not necessarily something bad. Far from it. The loss of self or the failure to be self is tragic, but the depression is more like a fever than a disease. It serves as a signal, a warning device that we have either been inhibited from developing some aspect of self or have been forced entirely too early to assume responsibilities we are not prepared to shoulder. Thus, children who can't be children when they're children may become depressed later in their lives because the child within has yet to find expression. Or, someone is led to believe and concurs in the belief that he or she is incapable of self-determination and thus chronically experiences depression. Were there no depression, no inner weight or pain, then a person could end up living out life to the end as inauthentic, unreal.

If the real demon "they" is to be exorcised, the self experiencing its own fever or warning signal of depression has somehow to be drawn out and made aware of possibilities and potentials yet to be realized. Someone who respects the inner worth and value of the person and isn't interested in making others into his or her own image and likeness is needed to model what it's like to author one's own life. Someone who draws attention over and over to the person's own capacity for thinking, feeling, and self-determination is needed to mirror what life is like without the shackles of "they." In "They," that someone is Jesus of Nazareth.

It is ironic that so many people have tried to be like Jesus of Nazareth rather than to be themselves as Jesus was himself. The man in "They" preferred to think and do as Jesus thought and did. This is not what Jesus wanted of him and it is probably not what he wants of those who follow him. The exorcism or healing that took place led the man to experience himself as himself in his thinking, feeling, and acting. Then and only then was he in a position to walk out of the synagogue with Jesus, not behind him.

Jesus models for all of us as the one who sets us free from the tyranny of "they," so that we too can model this for one another. How sad that, in the name of the Christ, so many people have been forced to deny what is unique in themselves. The man who was set free of the demon "they" was admonished to be vigilant because the same demon could come back at any time...and it surely has.

CHAPTER TWO
Reaching Out For Help

DEMONS

Mark 1:32-34: After sunset, as evening drew on, they brought him all who were ill, and those possessed by demons. Before long the whole town was gathered outside the door. Those whom he cured, who were variously afflicted, were many, and so were the demons he expelled.

At the crack of dawn while the village slept, they made their way to the place where Jesus was visiting. Some came with paper bags on their heads. Others had on phony noses and fake moustaches. Yes, some of the men even came disguised in women's dresses while some of the women had shoulder pads on under their sweaters and wore trousers so they'd look like men. Each had come alone because no one wanted anyone to know the reason for the visit. So, what a surprise it was to discover themselves in the courtyard of the home where Jesus was staying.

"Oh no!" one man gasped as he took the paper bag off his head and looked at the woman sitting across from him as she removed her beehive wig. "You mean you have a demon too? But you're my wife!"

"And you're my husband! You never told me you had a demon!" she exclaimed.

The man next to her took off his fake beard and stared in disbelief at his wife sitting across from him as she took off her fake beard as well. Together they asked "Have we both got demons?" and together they answered, "I guess we do."

All over the room people who had come in various sizes and disguises had surprises as they bumped into neighbors, friends, relatives, and associates. Over and over they found themselves saying, "You have to be kidding! You have a demon too? Well I never would have guessed it. How many times have we eaten together—had our bagels and lox—and not once did we suspect one another of having a demon."

Without knowing they would all be together, they had come intending to have Jesus expel their demons. As they waited in awkward silence for Jesus to appear, one lady dressed like a man spoke up. "Since we now know we all have demons, we might as well talk about them more openly to one another. After all, we have time. He can't really take care of our demons all at once; it surely will take time to expel all our demons even for such a powerful healer as Jesus."

So, as they sat there waiting, gradually they began to describe the demons that possessed them. One pot-bellied man with a few strands of hair on his head started out very quietly as he looked straight forward above the head of the woman across from him. He said he thought his demon was the suicidal thoughts that came into his head from time to time. He hadn't wanted to tell anyone he had that demon because he was afraid they would think he was crazy.

A woman in a floral-patterned house dress checked to see if the man who had just spoken had finished and then she cleared her throat. "I get so depressed. I don't feel like talking or walking. I just want to sleep all the time, and when I'm not sleeping, I eat donuts. So depression and overeating are my demons but I wouldn't tell anyone because I'm afraid people would think I was really off the wall."

"I get depressed too!" a young boy chimed in. "It's good to know someone else feels that way," he said with relief. "I'm afraid to tell my friends because they'd think I was a wimp."

"Well, I have to be strong so my family can lean on me and I don't feel very strong a lot of the time," a huge man with big hands and muscular arms and legs said softly. "My weakness is my demon and I'd be afraid to tell the other fellas that."

At first, the conversation stopped and started fitfully, lapsing into long silences, but as one, then two, then three villagers spoke up, more and more people wanted to speak. Husbands and wives shared their demons with one another; fathers and sons, mothers and sons, brothers and sisters. As one revealed his or her demons and the fear of speaking about them due to what others might think, everyone else listened with an understanding heart. Their understanding arose from having many of the same demons and fears themselves.

As they spoke, they gradually readjusted their chairs so they could see and hear one another more clearly. The pot-bellied man with the few strands of hair said, "I'm not as afraid as I was. I don't feel so anxious. I wonder if my demon has fallen asleep."

And the woman who ate so many donuts said, "I'm not as afraid as I was either. I think my demon must have gone out to lunch."

"My demon must have gone with yours," added the man with the big muscles. From all over the circle others talked about how they were less fearful.

Then the door opened and there in the archway he stood: the one for whom they had been waiting. He had a warm smile on his face and they all smiled back, expecting him to call them in one by one. But he did not. He surprised them by telling them they could go home because they had already been exorcised — their demons had been expelled and sent on their way!

"How can that be?" they said among themselves. Was he kidding them?

He motioned them to be quiet as he said, "Think back for a moment about what has just happened. Many of you have known one another for years. In some instances you have shared the same bed, the same office or table or playing field. Yet, you were unaware that each of you had your own special demon. And why was that? Because of your fear of admitting what you were going through. And that is your real demon! That is the demon which has paralyzed and cut you off from one another. That is the reason the demon has controlled you and had you in its power. The exorcism I have to offer, you have already experienced because you have come together and listened to one another as you have never done before. Your demon no longer controls you."

Then he told them that he had lots of work to do that day. They could all go, and as they left they could drop their disguises in the waste basket near the door. After all, they no longer had any need of disguises. Their demons had gone.

Reflection: Me And My Shadow

We may be inclined to laugh at all the disguises the people were wearing in "Demons." We laugh because the disguises are so obviously disguises: beehive wigs, fake moustaches, dresses for men, etc. What we don't realize is that we ourselves are walking around with our own disguises so that the people closest to us have no idea who is behind the mask. Carl Jung, the Swiss psychiatrist, referred to the mask we wear as the "persona." We want to appear acceptable to one another, so we do whatever we can to come off smelling like roses. Not only do we want to be acceptable to one another, we also have the need to be acceptable to ourselves. Therefore we may not permit ourselves to get in touch with what we consider a less desirable side of ourselves: namely, the shadow.

The shadow is the neglected side of the self. It is everything I think and feel that is contrary to my conscious way of seeing myself and contrary to how I want to be seen by others. Shadowy elements might be fear, resentment, strong sexual feelings, likes and dislikes that I cannot own or admit belong to me. Yet, the shadowy elements are mine; they are a dimension of me. As a matter of fact, they may be more me at times than the me I show to others. We cover our strong feelings of resentment towards someone with a smile or gesture of compliance that is just skin deep.

The people in "Demons" are possessed. They are victimized by their own personas. They can't let anyone see them without their masks. They have names for their various demons. Overeating, drinking too much, depression, harboring nasty thoughts toward spouses or children, etc., are the demons they name when they feel safe enough to talk. Jesus, however, tells them that the real demon is the fear they have of self-disclosure. And they finally came to terms with that demon in their confessions to one another. The unacknowledged and unowned fear was part of their shadow, which could only be owned once they removed their disguises, literally and figuratively, in an atmosphere of understanding acceptance.

Jesus does not need to heal them because mutual self-disclosure brings them into contact with one another's humanity, and their shared humanity is the healing activity. They no longer need to be secretive and protective about themselves since they can accept themselves as they are. They can be themselves without apologies.

The movement in this country to provide sanctuary in the churches for dissidents coming from Latin American countries is an admirable attempt to provide a place, a sacred space, for people who have lived in fear. It is unfortunate that we have not come to regard the church as the sacred space where all of us no longer need to flee in fear from our own personal demons and where we can be ourselves without the need for the variety of masks we bring to church. Hopefully, one day we shall experience the kind of exorcism each of the persons in "Demons" experienced as they listened to one another with understanding hearts.

Tuesday of the 4th Week of Lent

INSTALLMENTS

John 5:1-15: There was one man who had been sick for thirty-eight years. Jesus, who knew he had been sick a long time, said when he saw him lying there, "Do you want to be healed?"

Just about every afternoon anybody within earshot of Amos could hear the same question. "Will no one move me to the edge of the pool? How long do I have to lie here? Another thirty-eight years?" Yes, he had been lying there for thirty-eight years. But no one was certain whether he was forced to lie there or whether he really, deep down, wanted to be there. Of course, as far as Amos was concerned, he had no choice. "Every time the water starts moving, there is no one to help me into the pool. And when anyone finally does come, it's always too late!"

Others who knew Amos well had a different story. Mabel Silverstein, for one. A close friend of Amos', she was sharing her version of things to the Finkelsteins one afternoon while Amos was napping. "I have tried to help him any number of times," Mabel whispered to the retired couple, who had come to spend an hour with Amos. "One time I go up to him and I say 'Amos, Amos, the water is stirring. Let me help you over to the edge.' 'Are you kidding?' Amos says to me, 'I'm right in the middle of my prayers. I can't move in the middle of my prayers.' So I let him be. Well, by the time he is done with his prayers, he says 'I'm ready, I'm ready.' I say, 'You might be ready but the water isn't.' 'Too bad! Too bad!' he says back to me.

" 'Too bad.' I'll say it was too bad! And it was really too bad when a few days later I go up to him and say, 'Amos, Amos, the water is stirring. Let me help you over to the edge.' 'Are you kidding?' he says to me. 'I'm hallucinating!'

" 'Hallucinating what?' I ask him. 'I'm hallucinating that an angel of the Lord is talking to me, and the angel is telling me not to move a muscle at this time.' 'Why not?' I ask him. 'That I have not been told at this time. His instructions must come in installments!'

"Installments! Now you tell me what kind of nonsense is that? So I let him be. Well, by the time he is done with his hallucinating, he says, 'I'm ready, I'm ready' and I say, 'You might be ready but the water isn't.' 'Too bad, too bad' he says back to me.

"And then there was the time," Mabel is really animated now, "when I go up to him and say, 'Amos, Amos, the water is stirring. Let me help you over to the edge.' 'Are you kidding? I am waiting for my social security check and Mr. Social Security himself brings it. Should I be absent when he comes, it would be another month before he should come again and in the meantime what good is it if I am walking and have nothing to eat? I'd starve and die.' I look at him like he's lame not only in his legs but also in his head, but I let him be. Well, later he says, 'I'm ready, I'm ready.' 'So you're ready. You might be ready but the water isn't,' I say. 'Why are you always ready when the water isn't and versa-visa?' "

"Why do you think he is acting this way, Mabel?" asked Ruth Finkelstein. Mabel now raised her voice and spoke with the certainty born from hard experience. "I'm telling you, I think Amos doesn't want to get well! He just thinks he does."

"Why wouldn't he want to get well, Mabel? Who could want to stay sick for 38 years?" Ruth asks incredulously.

"Think about it, darling. If you had visitors bringing you bagels and lox every day, and people always looking after you, you might not want to give up a good thing either. I could be wrong, who knows? But some people like things the way they are even if it means living in misery. Well enough of that. I can see that Amos is waking up from his nap."

Mabel and the Finkelsteins moved closer to Amos till they were standing very near him. "Amos, honey, how do you feel today?" Mabel bent down and forced a smile. "Look who is here to see you today: The Finkelsteins."

"Moshe! Ruth! How nice to see you even if it is from the floor. But what difference does it make if I'm way down here and you're way up there? Just a little change in temperature!" Amos wisecracked as he pointed to some chairs. "Would you mind coming down to my level a bit? Not that I mind straining my lungs."

"Oh, we're sorry. Of course, we'll sit," Ruth apologized as she and Moshe sat down somewhat closer to Amos' level.

"That's better! Much better!" Amos said. "One of these days I'll be better. I'm not holding my breath, mind you. It's my hope, of course, that I'll fall into the pool before I fall into my grave. At least I'm hoping it will be in that order." The Finkelsteins didn't know whether to laugh or cry, Amos seemed so serious. Mabel just shook her head. She had been through all this before. "Enough is enough already," she muttered under her breath.

It was at that moment that something very strange happened: something that signaled a momentous change for Amos. Three young men made their way down the long corridor till they stood directly before Amos and his friends.

"How would you like to walk again?" one of the young men asked him abruptly.

"How would I like to walk again? Would a blind man like to see? Would a deaf man like to hear? Would a..."

The young man interrupted, "An angel of the Lord has entrusted me with the second installment of your instructions. You are now free to stretch your muscles and walk. You need not depend on anyone moving you to the pool, and you need not depend on anyone not moving you to the pool," he added cryptically.

Amos' mouth fell open in amazement. The second installment from the angel? How could that be? Then Amos laughed, thinking "There was never any angel! No instructions! I just told Mabel that so I could keep lying around the..." Amos' eyes opened wide as the reality hit him. He had made up that story about the angel. And he had probably made up many more stories just so he could keep lying around the pool day in and day out. Lying around the pool? He struggled to hold back his tears as he finally realized all the lying he had done—to himself and to Mabel and the others! But how did this perfect stranger in front of him know this story about the angel? What did he know that Amos himself had only now come to recognize?

"Well, how would you like to walk again?" The young man pressed Amos gently but firmly.

"I, I have no one to move me," Amos caught himself reaching for his old alibis. "Yes, I'm ready. I guess I'm ready."

The stranger continued, "Well, you can get up! You are healed!" He extended his hand to Amos who hesitated, and still wondering what was happening, gradually rose to his feet.

Everyone was amazed, especially Mabel. "Oy ve," she said. "I must be seeing things."

Amos took a few tentative steps forward. "Not bad, not bad at all," he muttered to himself. He then looked at the stranger suspiciously. "So the angel of the Lord gave you part two of the instructions?" His face brightened. "I am indebted to you for bringing this good news."

"I must go now," the stranger said, "but we shall meet again. There will be more to talk about, you can be sure." With that, the young man turned, rejoined his friends, and walked away. And Amos?

He turned to Mabel and the Finkelsteins with a look on his face that betrayed as much joy as embarrassment. He stepped forward and embraced Mabel.

When Mabel had gotten her breath, she whispered to Amos, "What are we going to do?"

"I don't know, Mabel, but I'm ready, I'm ready!"

Reflection:
It Pays To Be Sick

"Do you want to be healed?" Why would anyone who was
sick not want to be healed? This is the question Ruth
Finkelstein puts to Mabel. It is a question we can ask ourselves as well. Is there some area of our lives that needs healing
that we don't want healed? And if we don't, then why don't
we?

Some people are happy playing the role of the martyr. They
see themselves as perpetual victims. They think everyone is
out to get them, whether the others be relatives, friends,
grocers, politicians, etc. They need to play the role of victim
because in a perverse kind of way it makes them feel important. After all, everybody wants to get them. What would happen if they came to realize that others weren't especially
interested in them? Then they'd no longer be very special,
would they?

Then there are people who are angry. They have held on
to their grievances and their resentments for such a long
period of time that they wouldn't know who they were if they
were no longer angry or resentful. So who needs to be healed?

We also know of those who say they are paralyzed because
their parents prevent them from living their lives, or their
children demand all of their time, or their dog needs special
care. These are their reasons they give. But it is possible that
there is another reason, and that is all their reasons are con-
venient excuses for not assuming responsibility for living
their own lives. Only when that truth is faced—that their

paralysis is self-imposed—can the person stand up and walk into the future.

Any change in the status quo introduces some apprehension about the future. What will change bring? Will a person be worse or better off because of change? What will the person's newfound freedom lead to if the person is cured? Amos may seem to be a different animal from most of us. Yet, closer inspection shows us that he may very well be like us or we like him if the question Jesus put to him were put to us. "Do you want to be healed? Well?"

OVERRIPE

Mark 8:22-26: When they arrived at Bethsaida, some people brought him a blind man and begged him to touch him.

A bner was making his daily round of the produce merchants. "These bananas are very soft. Nobody's going to buy them if they feel this soft. And look—this one is already black." Abner's hands made their way to the peaches. "And these peaches. In one more hour they'll want to retire. They are downright mushy!" Moving to the grapes, he shook his head. "You call these grapes? They're all drying up!" Finally, Abner cautiously felt his way to where he thought the tomatoes were. Once there Abner gave one of the merchants some more of his free advice. "I don't mind telling you that these tomatoes are the closest thing to tomato soup outside the can that I can imagine."

Abner never convinced the merchants that what he had to say about their fruits or vegetables was true. For one thing, since he was blind Abner really couldn't tell what their produce looked like. Moreover, his whole method of testing whether the fruit or vegetables were salable was itself questionable. He would always squeeze the produce much harder than the merchants dared, and he left dents on all of the produce he examined.

However, the merchants were impressed with his determination to survive and his inventiveness in figuring out how. Long ago, they had decided among themselves to give him the benefit of the doubt and let him have some salable produce along with the unsalable so he could get along. They did more than this, though.

The merchants knew that Abner would take the fruit and vegetables, go five blocks down the street, and then set up his own little stand. There he would sell the fruit at half price by capitalizing on its overripe quality. Abner had quite a sales pitch too. "Overripe bananas for banana bread! Get your overripe peaches here...perfect for peach pie! A special on overripe apples for applesauce! Get high on fermenting pineapples! Buy your overripe tomatoes here. They are already half the way toward being good, healthy tomato soup!"

Most of the passersby just laughed. Occasionally, Abner would make a sale, but that was seldom. For the most part, it was the merchants themselves who came around and bought back the very fruit or vegetables they had given him just minutes earlier. Abner never realized what was up since he couldn't see them, and they disguised their voices. So it wasn't unusual for Abner to return to the merchants later in the day and talk them out of the very same produce he had gotten from them earlier! The merchants gladly conspired in this charade both because Abner was able to maintain his dignity and they were able to do what little they could for him.

When they heard one day that Jesus of Nazareth was in town, they thought they would be able to do even more for Abner. They knew of Jesus' remarkable powers, so they approached Abner to ask him if they could take him to be healed. They certainly didn't expect the answer they got.

"But I don't want to see! I'm happy the way things are, thank you." Abner was adamant.

"You don't want to see?" one of the merchants exclaimed. "But everybody wants to see. Surely you don't want to go around blind all your life if you have the chance to see?"

"Well, that is all well and good for you to say. But what would I do for a living if I could see?"

The merchants looked at one another. Abner had a point. But they also knew something he didn't: namely, how they were giving him produce and then buying it back so that he could survive. One of the merchants looked at the other merchants and then at Abner. He cleared his throat. "Abner, you have developed considerable skill determining whether our fruits and vegetables are overripe. You have a sense of touch like no one else! It seems to me," he continued as he winked at the others, "there might be a market for your talents. Have you ever thought of setting up a business to sell overripe fruits and vegetables for profit?"

Abner smiled slyly. "Well the thought has entered my mind from time to time."

"Just think of it," the merchant continued, "you could advertise soft apples as especially good for applesauce, soft peaches as good for peach pie, and so on."

"Not a bad idea," Abner acted as though he had never heard that line before. "And I could sell overripe tomatoes as the best kind for tomato soup, and old grapes as good for raisins!"

"Not a bad idea," the merchant agreed as though he hadn't heard that line before either. "I'm sure my fellow merchants would be willing to support you in this venture until you were on your own or, if you decided otherwise, to do something else." He looked around at the other merchants nodding their heads in silent agreement.

"Well now that that's settled," Abner said, feeling more relaxed about his future, "I think I'd like you to take me to Jesus. The truth is I've wanted to see for a long time but I've also been afraid—afraid that seeing would ruin my life. That's why I made no efforts to go to anyone who might help me."

The merchants looked at one another sadly. They knew their own well-intentioned scheme was partly responsible for keeping him in the dark. Now, in assuming the responsibility of helping Abner see, they would have to bear the full consequences of their decision. But they were resolved. Losing no time at all, they closed down their stalls and led Abner to Jesus to be cured of his blindness.

Jesus' eyes moved from the merchants to Abner and back again. "You have good friends," Jesus said, "friends who want you to see."

Abner nodded his head, "Yes, they want me to see, all right, even more than I seem to have wanted it, I'm ashamed to say. But I want to see now, really I do!"

"Good! Come with me," Jesus said as he led Abner by the hand. The two of them went some distance from the others.

Jesus put spittle on Abner's eyes and then laid his hands on him. There was silence for a minute. Then Jesus asked him if he saw anything. At first Abner saw nothing. Then gradually he began to experience light and the outline of objects he took to be trees.

"I can see people but they look like walking trees!" Abner exclaimed. Jesus put his hands on Abner a second time and this time Abner saw people and things clearly. "I can see! I can see!" he cried out.

"Yes, now you see." Jesus gazed deeply into Abner's newly opened eyes. "But there is much more you have yet to discover. You are still in the dark over many things in your life. When that darkness lifts, then your sight may bring you pain," Jesus left off explaining. "Now, however, is the time to celebrate with your friends! I've heard you sell overripe fruit. Do you have those soft peaches? They are a favorite of mine."

"I'll check with my partners." He winked. "But for you, I'm sure we can make a deal. You are my first customer!"

Reflection: Trapeze

If conversion experiences weren't painful, then no doubt more people would want to experience them. However, most people probably sense that any change as significant as conversion will involve pain,—the degree of pain depending on how radical the conversion and the temperament of the person undergoing it.

Why is conversion so painful?

Conversion is a transition from the known to the unknown. Someone has compared it to jumping from one trapeze to another. A person has to let go of one trapeze and plant his feet in midair before arriving at the next trapeze. When we move from one way of being to another, we move from what has provided security and stability in our lives and relationships to what may appear to be a chaotic future. It's true that, along with the stability and security, we have suffered and been cramped and ceased growing as persons. Yet, it is remarkable how we can live with suffering as long as we know we are safe. Husbands and wives will endure a bad marriage for a long period of time because their relationship has a certain predictability about it. And that is more than either of them can say about an unknown future without that relationship. Children may cling to abusive parents rather than move off into a foster home because they fear the unknown even more than the certain abuse.

An illustration of this resistance is Abner's admission that he really wanted to see but held back from seeking out Jesus because of his fear of a sighted but uncertain future. In conversion experiences, we want and we don't want to see. There is an approach/avoidance conflict. Whatever its source, the appeal to see is the appeal to an expansion of awareness, whereas the pull not to see is the temptation to hold back, retrench, and maintain the status quo. Abner was able to move forward only when he had the assurance of the merchants that there was hope for the future.

People don't change in a vacuum. Communal support sustains and nourishes a person going through difficult times, and communal indifference can make it almost impossible to change. Abner's friends' well-intentioned ploy to help highlights a very important lesson: what is good at one point in time may become destructive at another point. Supportive environments can become so comfortable that a person will never accept challenges to move beyond the environment without some kind of crisis precipitating movement. Communal support always runs the risk of over-protection, which makes conversion impossible.

CHAPTER THREE
The Healer's Credentials

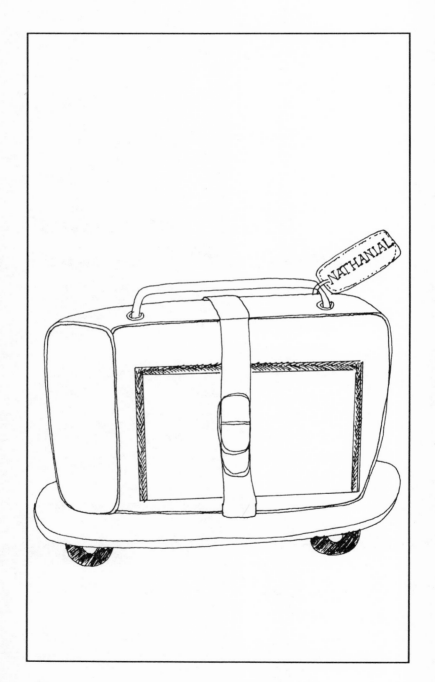

TRAVELING STICK

Luke 10:1-10: Do not carry a walking staff or traveling bag; wear
no sandals and greet no one along the way.

"Nat, we're to get our instructions in a couple of hours. I, for my part, am preparing for any eventuality." Standing in his apartment, Jude spoke with the confidence of a man who had carefully prepared for any assignment Jesus might give him.

"I can see. I can see," Nathanial said as he surveyed all that Jude had laid out on the floor.

Jude began listing his provisions. "You will notice I have a change of shorts for each day of the week. I also have two different tunics, each one being of a different color. Moreover, I have prepared five pairs of socks, two pairs of sandals and two capes. Should it be of a disposition to rain, one of the capes has been weatherproofed for just such an eventuality." Jude paused to appreciate the wisdom of weatherproofing his cape. Then he continued, "You will also see there on the floor, between my flashlights and toolbox, a safety kit complete with Band-Aids, scissors, Mercurochrome, and a can of mosquito repellent, economy size."

"I see. I see," Nathanial said as he tried to follow Jude's guided tour of his preparations for the journey. Jude spoke with the assurance of an expert as he said, "You will also notice I have candy bars in reserve as well as cereal to eat without milk if such be the need. I will not take the time to more than mention that I have dehydrated chicken soup packets sewn into the lining of my weatherproofed cape so we will not starve if by accident we should meet with robbers on the road." The thought hadn't crossed Jude's mind that if the robbers stole the cape, they would also get the packets of soup.

"Very smart, very smart," Nathanial said more out of respect than as a comment on Jude's foresight.

"As for my traveling bag, no doubt you have heard of Samsonite? Well, my friend, I have the newest in luggage from the same company that makes Samsonite and this luggage is called Son of Samsonite! I wouldn't settle for anything less. I have here two pieces, one of which is bigger than the other. They are both here underneath the bed. Please look."

"I see. I see," Nathanial said as he got down on his knees alongside of Jude to admire the ruby red pieces of Son of Samsonite luggage stored safely beneath the bed.

"I must tell you that the smaller piece of luggage has a special compartment for two or three books on tips for travelers. These tips, mind you, range all the way from suggestions on what to do when you are mugged to how to behave in the houses you visit so as to be invited back again. You never can be prepared enough for what may happen on a journey," Jude stated confidently.

"So true. So true," Nathanial said with less than total honesty. He wasn't sure about the value of these tips for travelers, but he wasn't going to argue the point with Jude.

"Finally," Jude sounded as though the tour were coming to an end, "in the bigger piece of luggage there is a special feature I call my magic bar."

"Your magic bar?" Nathanial's curiosity was aroused.

"Yes. Please stand back and I will show you." Jude rolled up his sleeves and pressed a small button on the little compartment door in the suitcase. As Nathanial looked on in astonishment, a door magically opened and a tray that seemed endless emerged from the compartment. On the tray was an assortment of schnapps and a miniature bucket of ice. "You have heard of 'one for the road,' no doubt. Well, I believe in one and then some—on the road!" he said by way of commentary on the usefulness of his magic bar.

As Nathanial shook his head, it wasn't clear whether he thought the magic bar was the result of wise planning or the product of a weird mind. However, Jude was too engrossed in what he had been doing to bother with anything Nathanial might be thinking.

"So you see, Nat, when we see Jesus and get our traveling instructions, I am of the opinion that Jesus may even shake his head in wonder and admiration at what I have done to prepare myself."

"Oh, you can be sure of that. You can be sure of that," Nathanial said as he stroked his beard and imagined Jesus' reaction to all of this. "But get your stuff together, Jude. We have to be on our way. Jesus wants to meet all of us in thirty minutes in front of Abe's Corner Bar."

"No problem," Jude said as he methodically and quickly returned everything to the suitcases. Nathanial guessed that Jude had practiced packing and unpacking because he seemed to know exactly where everything went. With a final sweep of the room, Jude locked his grips, set them on what looked like small skateboards, and started pulling them by means of long straps towards the door. "I'm ready. Let's go."

When Jude and Nathanial arrived at the corner in front of the bar, most of the other disciples had already gathered. Jude was mildly surprised that he was the only disciple who was so well prepared. Perhaps, he thought to himself, the others simply didn't have his foresight. Or perhaps they had left what they were taking with them in the bar while they waited for Jesus.

Within a couple of minutes Jesus arrived at the corner and the group was complete. All the disciples gathered around him. Jude, however, had a little problem hauling his Son of Samsonite luggage into the huddle and had to remain in the back.

Jesus counted noses to be sure all of the disciples were present. Seeing they were, he began. "I'm going to be sending you off two by two, fellas, and this is how you are to go. I don't want you to take any change of clothes, any money, any food, any luggage, or any change of sandals. But you are welcome to take a traveling stick." Jesus had no sooner finished speaking than they all heard a loud thud at the back of the huddle.

They all turned and there was Jude on the ground. He had collapsed next to his luggage. Philip bent down and slapped him gently on either cheek. As Jude slowly came to, he kept muttering, "A traveling stick. Only a traveling stick? I have everything *but*, and everything *but* is what he doesn't want!"

Once he had been helped to his feet, Jude looked at Jesus with a hurt look. "I'm not one to deny my faith in you, Jesus. Never have I questioned you. But that our provisions should be no more than a traveling stick! This I cannot understand. How are we going to manage without a change of clothes? How will we survive without candy bars? Without 1001-handy-tips-to-avoid-being- mugged, and knowing-what-to-say-and-what-not-to-say-in-trying- circumstances? And how can we possibly get along without a magic..." Jude caught himself. He was going to say, "a magic bar," but then realized that this would not help his case very much. "Forget about that last item," Jude said waving his hand in the air. "But just please tell me why we can only take a traveling stick with us? And while you're at it, just what are we supposed to do with a stupid traveling stick? If it's for support, I must tell you that offhand I can think of one hundred things I would prefer to a dumb traveling stick."

Jesus didn't try to defend his instructions. He didn't ask Jude why Jude needed what he needed for traveling. Indeed, he even agreed that the traveling stick sounded kind of silly. "Why take only a traveling stick? Well, the whole point of going on the journey with nothing is that all you would have to fall back on when you were with others would be yourselves. You wouldn't be able to impress people with anything you had—just with who you are. They'd accept you or reject you for yourselves. Because the only thing you'd have to offer would have nothing to do with clothes, books, impressive credentials, or fast talk. But Jude, maybe you're right. Why take a traveling stick? Someone might even try to impress people with that....twirling it around like a baton, they might forget that the kind of healing you came to do was simply to be with them as yourself. You have a point, Jude. I change my instructions. Fellas, no traveling sticks! I send you as you are. And it is through you as you are that others will come to be healed. It is through your presence that they will come to know the power of God."

Jude had regained his composure by this time and as they dispersed he stopped one of the passersby near the city gates. "Would you like to buy some Son of Samsonite luggage? It has a magic bar!"

The disciples were on their way.

Reflection: Real Presence

In our age, the age of specialization, we may prefer to leave healing to the professionals: the medical doctors and nurses, the psychologists, psychiatrists, social workers, ministers or priests—in short, people who have special training and special equipment for that kind of thing. Those of us who aren't professional feel particularly at a loss. Without credentials, what can we do for those who need healing?

Jude does not live in an age of specialization. But he certainly feels the need to be well prepared for the journey he and the other disciples are taking into the villages. There they will be expected to help people, perhaps even to heal them. So Jude readies himself as best he can for any problem that may present itself on the trip. What he isn't prepared for are Jesus' instructions.

And the point of Jesus' instructions is that preparation can get in the way of what the disciples are really supposed to be doing in the towns they visit. Just as today we can rely too heavily on techniques, how-to-say-the-right-thing manuals, and gimmicks, so Jude and the others can easily rely too much on what is of secondary importance on the journey.

According to Jesus, the indispensable tool for healing is the self: the compassionate self in all its imperfection. That self, stripped of all pretense and game playing, is the most valuable asset of any healer. One recovering alcoholic helps another in and through admitting to be a recovering alcoholic. The mother whose son has died of AIDS may very well be the source of healing to another whose son or daughter has died of AIDS. It is the healer's still-wounded self that alone speaks to the other's wound. Wound consciousness is vital if healing is to take place.

No one can be excused from carrying out some kind of healing. We cannot exempt ourselves because we are too young or too old, too ignorant or too educated. Some of us hold back because we don't think we have enough to say or fear we'll say it poorly. But that is no excuse, for it is presence, human presence that heals, and not smooth-sounding words. People confined to hospital beds or nursing homes or hospices are more in need of good listeners than of good speakers. And those who have recently lost a loved one are not making mental notes about the vocabulary or diction of those who visit and offer their sympathy.

Jesus knows what he is doing when he sends his disciples out almost naked. They have nothing to fall back on but themselves and the assurance that he will be with them. What more can they, or we, want?

THE NAG

Luke 18:1-8: He told them a parable on the necessity of praying always and not losing heart: "Once there was a judge in a certain city who respected neither God nor man. A widow in that city kept coming to him saying, 'Give me my rights against my opponent.'"

He had had a long day. There were an unusually large number of cases, so he had spent less time than ever in reaching his judgments. Not that he had ever really spent much time on any of the cases that came before him. He was never all that interested, and when he was you could bet there was a little money in it for him. It never hurt a plaintiff to have a few shekels on hand for a quick or favorable decision from this judge. He didn't drive a Lincoln Continental on his salary. No, the people's appreciation for what he had done on the bench financed his cars, his cottages, and his cruises. Of course "the people's appreciation" was simply another name for bribery.

The judge was ready to call it quits for the day. It was already late afternoon and everyone appeared to have left the courtroom. Doodling pad in hand, he started to rise from his chair when he heard someone say, "Mr. Judge, Mr. Judge, you've got to hear me out!" He halted and peered over the rims of his glasses into the echoing courtroom. There stood a lady in her mid-sixties alone before the bench. She couldn't have been more than 5' 4" tall and weighed all of ninety pounds at most.

"I'm sorry, Mrs...."

"Mrs. Maier, but you can call me Mitzi."

"I'm sorry, er, Mitzi, but we close at 5:00 P.M."

"But Mr. Judge, it is only ten minutes to five. You have ten more minutes, and this will only take two. Please, oh please, your honor." He was about to order her to leave when she added coyly, "You have a reputation for being so kind."

He hadn't heard anyone tell him that before. He didn't really buy it, but he couldn't say no to her request, not yet. "OK. You have two minutes," he said as he repositioned his doodling pad, sat down, clicked his pen to attention, and waited.

"Well, Mr. Judge, it's about our landlord. He's trying to evict ten people from our building who can't pay the terribly high rent he wants. And..."

"And who is your landlord?" he interrupted.

"Abe Muskowitz, Mr. Judge."

Though the judge appeared not to know the landlord, Abe Muskowitz had come to his courtroom before. In fact he deeply appreciated the judge. About a month ago they had reached a decision very favorable to Abe. And the following week the judge had an expensive new suit of clothes, compliments of Abe Muskowitz. "Well, I'll tell you Mitzi, let's say you come here in six weeks and I'll see what I can do. By that time, all the paperwork should be taken care of."

"Six weeks! Oy ve!" Mitzi sounded horrified. "In six weeks those tenants will be out on the streets. Can't you do it earlier, Mr. Judge?"

"Well, maybe four weeks." The judge decided to let her think she was getting a deal.

"Four weeks. Oh, Mr. Judge. Four weeks of suffering, four weeks of uncertainty, four weeks of..."

"That's enough, Mrs. Maier." The rap of the gavel was meant to be conclusive. "We will see you in four weeks. Have a good day." The judge gathered up his day's doodlings and left the courtroom.

Mitzi was left standing there, her arms lifted high, staring at the door through which the judge had vanished, "All right, Mr. Judge, we'll see who is going to have a good day."

In his chambers the judge took off his black robes and stood for a minute admiring his doodling. "Not bad! Not bad! Now for a little tea," he thought as he rang the bell on his desk.

As he continued comparing today's doodles with yesterday's, the door opened and a voice called out, "Tea time, Mr. Judge. And by the way, four weeks is just too long. Would you want to see ten poor homeless people begging at your front door day in and day out?"

The judge wheeled around and there was Mitzi with an apron around her waist and a pot of tea in her hands. "What are you doing here?" the judge asked in surprise.

"Finishing our little talk!" Mitzi answered.

"Our little talk is over until four weeks from now," the judge said as he pointed to the door. "And I don't want to see you until then. Please go and leave me alone."

"But Mr. Judge" Mitzi pleaded.

"Go!"

"Ok. Ok. So they have nowhere to sleep. So they freeze to death."

"Freeze? It's the middle of the summer!"

"I can't help it if they've got thin blood."

"Go!" He took Mitzi by the elbow, ushered her out of the chambers, and locked the door behind her. "Pest!" he said as he sat down to his tea. Unfortunately, there was no tea, just hot water. "That's it!" he said out loud. "I'm going home!" Warily he unlocked and opened the chamber door. She was gone. He was through the courtroom and halfway down the hallway when he decided to freshen up before driving home.

When he entered the restroom, he spotted an attendant there dressed in a white coat and white pants. "Hmmmmmmm," he thought to himself, "they're getting pretty classy in here. I've never seen the workers dressed like this before."

Just as he was about to enter one of the stalls, he heard a voice whine, "And how would you like it if the tenants picketed your house with signs that read, 'Mr. Judge has sentenced us to death'? So ten people starve to death because of you. So what does it matter to you?"

The judge slammed the stall door behind him and yelled, "What are you doing here? Do you want to get arrested?"

"What for?" Mitzi said innocently. "For looking after ten people whom you are starving to death, people with no heat and not even a stall to call their own?"

"But they don't need heat in the middle of the summer. And they aren't starving. And as for the stall—"

"Sure, easy for you to say, Mr. Judge. You don't have thin blood!"

The judge bolted from the stall, washed his hands, pressed the buzzer for the electric drier to dry his hands and waited in vain for it to start up. He then looked for paper towels and could find none.

Mitzi hoped he was learning a lesson. "So now you're getting the idea of what it's like to be without."

The judge was beside himself as he wailed, "Nag, nag, nag!" and in his panic to flee the restroom, he accidentally ran into the broom closet. When he finally got out, he shot as fast as he could to the parking lot and his Lincoln Continental.

The judge hopped into his car but as luck would have it, he found a little old Pinto had parked him in. "Now whose car is that? Who could possibly have parked in such a dumb way?" He didn't have long to puzzle that one out.

"Well, now, isn't this a coincidence?" Mitzi emerged from her Pinto. He recognized the voice and he slumped over into the passenger seat. "My little Pinto. Not a Lincoln Continental but it will do. It will do. Now Mr. Judge, as I was saying before you left the men's room, who is going to pay for the burials?"

"What burials?" But the judge knew he shouldn't have asked.

"Those ten poor people you threw out!"

"But they're not dead and I didn't throw them out."

"So why argue about details? It's just a matter of time."

"Oh God, what did I do to deserve this? Tell me, tell me!"

"Who needs God to tell you this? I will do. I will do," Mitzi said with self-assurance.

That was all the judge needed to hear. He jumped out of his car and started walking fast, very fast, down the street. Mitzi kept after him. "Mr. Judge, it isn't fair that you should be pushing old women like me around. It isn't fair that you are thinking of starving all the homeless!" By this time, people on the street were following what was happening with considerable interest. They all started following the judge and Mitzi as Mitzi's voice got louder and louder. After six blocks, the judge was out of breath and had to stop. Mitzi, on the other hand, seemed to grow stronger the further she walked and the more people who joined their little parade.

When she finally caught up with the judge, she dropped down on the curb beside him and started weeping about their children and all the years he hadn't paid for their support.

"She's crazy, she's crazy!" he thought. "I'll do anything, anything to get her off my back." Then he looked at Mitzi and said, "All right, all right. We shall take care of this matter tomorrow at 9:00 A.M. in the courtroom!"

"Promise, Mr. Judge?"

"I promise."

"Cross your heart and hope to die?"

"Yes, yes, cross my heart and hope to die."

Mitzi looked at him, patted him on the head and said, "No wonder they say you are such a kind man." Then she looked up at the sky, smiled and said, "We won, Lord, we won!"

Reflection:
Through Others' Eyes

They are not nice people to have around, these people who nag. They whine, pester, never let up, make nuisances of themselves, meet you at every turn, disturb your peace, and eventually drive you crazy. They can also make you feel guilty, angry, out of sorts, even homicidal. What do they care provided they get what they are after! Mitzi is a nagger, a first class nagger. And what she wants is justice.

Can we picture ourselves in that role? Nagging others for justice's sake might prove a more difficult role than we first thought. Certainly, we would run into opposition. Whether we'd feel like cornering them in restrooms or doggedly keeping after them on side streets as they got angrier and angrier is something worth pondering before we get too excited about the role. We know what happened to naggers like Martin Luther King, the Berrigans, and others who wouldn't let up. And we're aware of what happens to those involved in finding sanctuary for our Central American brothers and sisters when they nag for justice's sake. Yes, maybe we ought to rethink our desire for the role of nagger and settle for the more comfortable one of the unjust judge, a role we may already have practiced enough to play reasonably well. But that doesn't mean we are off the hook. Not by any means.

If we consciously take on that role, then we had better be prepared to suffer being nagged. After all, the judge was bothered; all the nagging got to him. He couldn't rest and he was disturbed. If we could really let ourselves be bothered and upset so that we felt we were cornered and had to do something about the injustices we were responsible for, then maybe taking on that role would be a step in the right direction.

But where is the healing in all of this? It is in the empathic response. Empathy is the ability to identify with others and to experience life as they do to the degree that is possible. Mitzi gets under the judge's skin and is an irritant, but she does that because first she has been able to place herself in the skin of the people whose case she pleads. She is not a cool, detached observer who makes her report and then departs from the scene of those who suffer. No, she is one with them and in her solidarity is moved to action. What is healing in empathy is the attunement of the self to the other self or selves. What flows from the empathic response may lead to some kind of advocacy (for example, on behalf of minorities, women, abused children, the elderly), or it may mean sitting quietly and holding a dying person's hand. Always, however, it is being with and not simply being for someone. For unless we know the angle of perception, the manner in which the other sees, hears, feels, and tastes, we may end up satisfying our own needs rather than the needs of the other.

It is important that we realize the distinction between empathy and pity. Pity is condescending; empathy is not. No one who has a sense of his own worth or dignity wants pity because pity is the relationship of a subject (the one who pities) to an object (the one pitied). Empathy, on the other hand, is the relationship of subject to subject in which one person enters into the suffering or joy of another to experience that suffering or joy as the other experiences it.

When we read of Jesus that he is the lamb who takes away the sin of the world, perhaps we have here an illustration of the empathic response. Jesus enters into the pain and brokenness of others and in so doing alleviates that pain. Alleviating the pain is not removing it but making it bearable, because those who suffer know now that they are not isolated and alone in what they are going through. Taking away sin, then, is fully entering into it ("he became sin for us") without necessarily removing it.

Anyone who practices the empathic response is well on the way to being a practitioner in healing.

Power

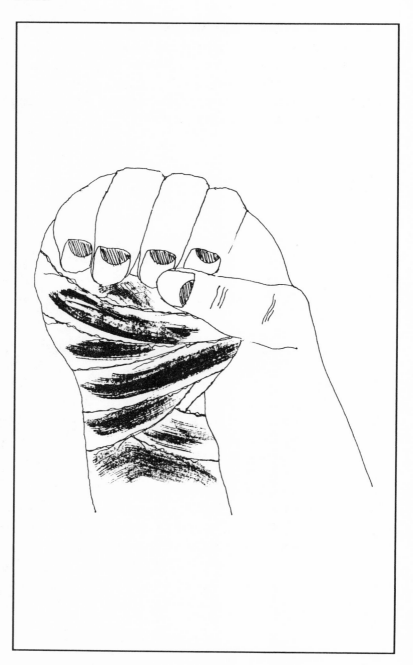

POWER

Matthew 8:1-4: ....Suddenly a leper came forward and did him homage, saying to him, "Sir, if you will to do so, you can cure me."

He had never been much to look at to begin with—an egg-shaped head, eyes that seemed too close together, separated only by a paper-thin nose. Age had given him wrinkles deep as canyons and had taken his teeth, leaving a gaping hole for a mouth that almost swallowed his chin. He was so stooped that when he walked he saw mostly other peoples' feet and rarely, if ever, their faces. No, he had never been much to look at, but now no one looked. In fact they turned their faces or fled in horror, what with the snow-white skin, the running sores, and, most noticeable, the stumps that once were hands and feet.

In one way he was like so many others on that small plot of land set aside for them outside the city. But in another way he was very different. For he had never known what it was like to have another hold his hand, caress his face, or slip a loving arm around him. The others could at least sustain themselves with memories of happier times during their ever-present loneliness. But Naaman, partly because he had never been much to look at and partly because he had fallen ill so young, never felt that anyone ever had or ever could care for him.

It was the custom of their little community in the evening to gather up and share whatever food passersby had left them. They ate their food in silence, one sitting on a stump, some on the ground, others huddled around the fire—but all preoccupied with the hunger and the loneliness unique to each.

So they really didn't notice the stranger among them that evening. Even had they noticed, they would have thought him to be another like themselves. After all, what healthy person in his right mind would come to this place? Certainly, Naaman, stooped as he was, hadn't noticed him. Besides, it seemed to him pointless and painful to look up in the faces of the others only to see reflected there the loneliness that he knew all too well.

The stranger had propped himself against the same huge boulder as Naaman. Slowly eating his piece of bread, Naaman heard what sounded like sobbing. It wasn't loud, but still it was noticeable. Naaman didn't pay much attention to the crying, for he had heard it all before—and all too frequently. Occasionally, the sobs were punctuated with sighs as though the stranger were experiencing inner turmoil. Naaman had heard sighs like these before too, but for some reason he found himself putting down his piece of bread and listening carefully. What surprised him most was that he felt drawn to extend his gnarled hand to the stranger. He stopped himself, so conditioned was he to expect any offer of tenderness to be viewed as repulsive. As he withdrew his hand, he saw the stranger's hand reach out to his. Much to Naaman's surprise, the stranger clasped his hand and held it close to his chest. Though it was dark, Naaman could tell by the feel of the skin on the stranger's hand that he was not one of them.

The stranger began to speak. He told of his impending death at the hands of those whom he had come to help; of how it was inevitable because of the jealousy of those in power; of how lonely and misunderstood he felt at times. Yet, he also spoke with conviction about how he needed to do what his father wanted him to do. Naaman understood his loneliness but very little else. All he could do was lend the stump of his hand to the stranger who seemed to need some human tenderness even more than Naaman did.

The stranger's voice grew calm. Naaman detected a newfound serenity. Finally the stranger thanked Naaman as he massaged his battered hand. Then he lifted the stump to his lips and kissed it reverently. He released the hand as if he were returning a precious treasure. As the stranger rose, he lifted Naaman to his feet, took him in his arms, and held him close. In that instant Naaman felt as though he were standing straight even though he continued to stoop; he felt beautiful even though his face stayed unchanged; he felt whole even though his fingerless hands remained unchanged. Naaman wanted to yell out, to thank him, to let him know how grateful he was, but he was too overjoyed to speak. By the time his mind had cleared, the stranger had left. Yet, he felt he had to say or do something; he could not contain himself!

Naaman hobbled back to the others. Although he could hardly see their faces, Naaman recognized them by their sobs. As best he could, Naaman smiled down at one of those who was weeping, put his arms around him and held him tight. In that embrace, both lepers began to smile and come alive with some newfound power. Then both Naaman and the other leper reached out to others and embraced them. It was only a matter of minutes before the lepers were all embracing one another!

That night a power was shared among the lepers, a power they had never felt before. A healing took place the likes of which no one there had ever witnessed! And even though nothing physically changed for the lepers, nothing remained the same. And no one was more aware of how that change had come than Naaman.

Reflection:
This And That

An infirmity of one kind or another marks the person who is in need of healing. There is a weakness or a deficiency that needs tending and caring. Physicians mend their patients' bodies, while psychiatrists look after their client's minds. Priests and ministers care for the souls of distressed parishioners. Men and women bring words of consolation to the lonely in nursing homes, hospital wards, and prisons. The infirm who are healed are strengthened and made whole at least temporarily if not permanently. We could easily conclude, then, that in any healing activity there is one who heals and one in need of healing. But is this really true?

Consider the proposition that there is interdependence in all interaction between and among persons as well as between and among everything in creation. If I teach, I can only do so because there is a student who receives my teaching; if I preach, it is only possible because there are those there to receive my word and who in turn nourish me through their own feedback. Mothers can be mothers to the extent that children are receptive and open to being mothered, and mothers know the pain of finally being told, "Don't mother me anymore!" Chairs become chairs to the extent they are sat upon and people become sitting people only because there are chairs to receive them. Stars and celebrities shine because there are those among us who sigh, "ooh" and "ahh." Interdependence means mutuality, reciprocity, give and take.

The story "Power" dramatically illustrates that healing is also interdependent. Naaman appears to be the wounded one, but he experiences healing power going outside of himself to Jesus, who is the healer. Naaman experiences himself as healer and healed in one and the same act. Likewise, although we do not have Jesus' subjective response to what holding Naaman's hand did for him, we might safely conclude on the basis of Jesus' newfound serenity that he too is healed in the action of healing Naaman. It should be pointed out that neither of them heal from a position of power nor for that matter from a position of powerlessness. Rather they heal out of their woundedness, which is paradoxically their weakness and their strength: the locus of their powerlessness and of their power. Thus, they relate to one another neither out of need nor out of self-sufficiency but out of both. They are interdependent. And through their interdependence they can become more fully themselves in one another's presence.

It is safe to conclude, then, that healing is an interdependent activity and that the medium of the healing is the wound, a source of neither power or powerlessness but both. The recovering alcoholic through his wound reaches out to another alcoholic whose own wound permits him to heal; the widow whose husband has died a year ago understands better than anyone else her neighbor's grief on the death of her husband. Wound speaks to wound, and in that dialogue people heal and are healed by one another.

CHAPTER FOUR
The Healer's Therapy

THE GIFT

Mark 5:21-24; 35-43: "The child is not dead. She is asleep."

Everyone has a gift, a talent. Rachel had one too. "I can hold my breath. I can hold my breath a long time, longer than anybody." Yes, everybody has a gift. However, that doesn't mean that everybody else recognizes or appreciates it. That would be nice, but sometimes it just doesn't happen that way. "I can hold my breath. I can hold my breath a long time, longer than anybody," Rachel bragged to anyone who listened.

"Isn't that nice," Rachel's grandma said.

"Isn't that nice," Rachel's uncle said.

"Isn't that nice," Rachel's teachers said.

Rachel wondered just how nice they really thought it was that she could hold her breath a long time, longer than anybody else. For after saying, "Isn't that nice," Rachel's grandma, uncle, and her teachers never bothered to ask her how she could hold her breath so long or what she hoped holding her breath would accomplish. They didn't ask anything at all. Clearly, not everybody really recognized Rachel's gift.

The next question is: Did anybody, anybody at all, recognize just how tremendous it was that she could hold her breath a long time, longer than anybody? She had hoped her mom or her dad could appreciate it. She would run up to her mom and blurt, "Look, mom, I can hold my breath." Quickly she'd inhale, and her cheeks would swell as she closed her eyes and held her breath.

Well, her mom would simply say, "Rachel, stop it! I don't want to see you do that again. Do you understand?"

Rachel's cheeks would deflate like leaky balloons and she would walk away sad because her mom didn't notice her gift. As for her dad, Rachel would go to her dad when he was poring over his books. She would beam at him and ask, "Do you wanna know what I can do better than anyone else, daddy?"

"Not now, Rachel. I have a lot of work to do. Maybe later. Come back later."

So Rachel would wait and wait. Then she would return to her father's study. "Can I show you now, daddy, huh? Do you wanna see what I can do better than anyone else? Huh?"

"Rachel, come back in half an hour. Then you can tell me," her father would say without looking up from his books.

Well, Rachel had heard that line so many times before, she didn't believe it anymore. So she would run off to her brothers and ask them the same question she had asked her father. She would interrupt them as they played, "Do you wanna know what I can do better than anyone else?"

"We already know," they'd say. "You can make a pest out of yourself better than anybody else!"

With a hurt look in her eyes Rachel would answer, "Well, I didn't want to tell you anyway. So there!"

After that, she would try her sisters. "Rachel, that's silly! What's so great about holding your breath?" Rachel's sisters shook their heads as they looked at her.

Rachel was particularly sad because not even her friends thought she had a gift. They always used to make her stop.

"Rachel, if you hold your breath like that, you could get big and fly away," they'd say to her. Or, "Rachel, if you hold your breath that long, you will bust open and all your insides will come out!"

Of course Rachel didn't believe her friends. As far as she was concerned, she had a gift. She could hold her breath, longer than anybody else. Even if no one else seemed to think holding breath was important, she did. And every time she was by herself, she practiced holding her breath. She became so good at it that she could do it without seeming to do it at all. No longer did her cheeks get big and puffy when she inhaled, her eyes didn't bulge, and her face no longer turned all red. Rachel was happy with her gift and she always thanked God for it.

Now as is often the case with people who have gifts or talents, they come to use their gifts almost unconsciously. This is what happened to Rachel. "I can hold my breath while I'm asleep," she said to her cat, since her cat was the only creature alive who bothered to listen to her. "I really can," she reassured the cat.

Rachel had in fact gotten so good at holding her breath, she could lie motionless for hours as if she were dead. "I might as well be dead, since nobody pays much attention to me anyway," she thought. "Maybe if I held my breath and played at being dead, others would finally notice." The plan was hatched.

The next morning she decided to stay home from school and play at being sick. No need to rush into playing dead all at once! After she had played at being sick for a couple of days her grandma, her uncle, her teachers, relatives, and friends all came to visit her. This was great! After a few days of playing at being worse and loving the attention that brought, Rachel decided it was time to play at being dead. "I think I'll play at being dead. Then I'll really be well off."

And, of course, Rachel had this gift no one knew about because no one had ever cared to know. So, Rachel sneaked a deep breath one day when one of her sisters came to visit. Rachel appeared to be dead. Rachel's sister was beside herself. She ran out of the room and cried the news to Rachel's mother. Rachel's father wasn't at home because he had gone into the village to find Jesus of Nazareth. He had heard of Jesus' healing powers and wanted him to cure his daughter. Rachel's mother was grief stricken and ordered one of the servants to get Rachel's father. Rachel couldn't get over just how powerful her gift was. She thought she would hold her breath just as long as she could if it meant getting all this attention.

An hour had passed when Rachel heard her relatives arguing in the next room. "What do you mean, 'she isn't dead but alive'?! How can you say that?" they said, laughing with a cruelty Rachel recognized.

"She is asleep. That is all. Let me into the room." Rachel stiffened as she heard those words. The voice was gentle but firm. "Let me see her alone—at least for a minute."

There was silence and then Rachel felt her hand slip into someone else's hand. "Rachel, Rachel," the voice began. It was the same gentle voice she had heard a minute earlier. "Did anyone tell you that you have a great gift for holding your breath a long time, longer than anybody else? Has anyone ever said to you, 'Rachel, you must have a good set of lungs and a good heart to hold your breath so long!'"

Rachel opened one eye and peeked at the stranger who held her hand. "No," she whispered. "No one has ever told me that."

"Well, I am here to tell you. And it is a wonderful gift, too. One day you may be able to save people from drowning because you can hold your breath so long. Why, I bet with all the breath you're able to store up, you'll be able to blow out big fires one day. Who knows? You could even sing the national anthem on one breath load. But first you have to come back to life."

Rachel opened her other eye.

"We want a live little girl with your ability, not a dead one," Jesus said with a smile. And when Jesus smiled, Rachel thought it probably would be better to be a live little girl who could hold her breath rather than a dead one. Then Jesus took her by the hand and said, "Get up, Rachel," and as she stood up, he added, "I bet you're starved! How about having something to eat?" Jesus led her to her astonished parents and told them, "Rachel is alive, but..." and here he winked at Rachel, "...don't hold your breath waiting for an explanation. Just get her a glass of milk and some cookies."

Rachel smiled. Finally, someone knew the gift she had!

Reflection:
Look, Ma! No Hands!

Dr. Heinz Kohut was a psychiatrist who founded the school of psychology called Self psychology. What Kohut emphasized over and over again in his writings was the importance of positive parental mirroring of children. He maintained that babies and little children display a normal, healthy grandiosity, and that they need to have that grandiosity mirrored back to them. For example, a child comes into the room on his tricycle and shouts "Look, Ma! No hands!" It is important that he or she get rave reviews from mom and not an unresponsive silence or a "Don't bother me now." The mirroring approval from mom, "Wow, that's great!" lets him know that he counts and matters. Her response serves as an affirmation of his being. If she decides to withhold that approval, then it is a statement to him that he doesn't count—or worse, that he just doesn't exist.

"The Gift" is a story about a little girl who has a gift: a gift that needs to be affirmed. Obviously, Rachel displays some of the grandiosity just mentioned, claiming that she can hold her breath, longer than anybody else. Yet that gift isn't acknowledged, and when any mention is made of it, Rachel is not praised but admonished and made to feel unwanted. She thanks God for her gift, but like all of us she needs to be affirmed by other human beings.

That she should have to practice playing dead to get the attention of others is a sad commentary not only on the lack of positive mirroring in her life but also a statement about the meaning of suicide in the lives of others. For some, suicide seems to be a way of saying, "I don't count and I'm not noticed now, but if I kill myself and remove myself from your lives, then you will know I was around."

Rachel's healing takes place because Jesus entered the room and took the time to mirror her own grandiose needs. He didn't analyze the need nor did he say she ought to be more realistic. He participated in the fantasy and let her know just how important holding her breath was; he also managed to bring her back to the land of the living. She could best use her talent as a live little girl, not as a dead one.

We might be inclined to think that overdoing praise is downright unhealthy. Kohut tells us that when children do not receive the mirroring they need, they become adults who never get enough praise and always need the approval of others for what they do and who they are. Only with early, adequate mirroring do we become capable of self mirroring later on. Another word for this self mirroring is self-esteem. There is no need to be cheap when it comes to affirming children, or adults for that matter. Jesus brought a little girl back to life by doing it, and in our own way we too can help people come back to life.

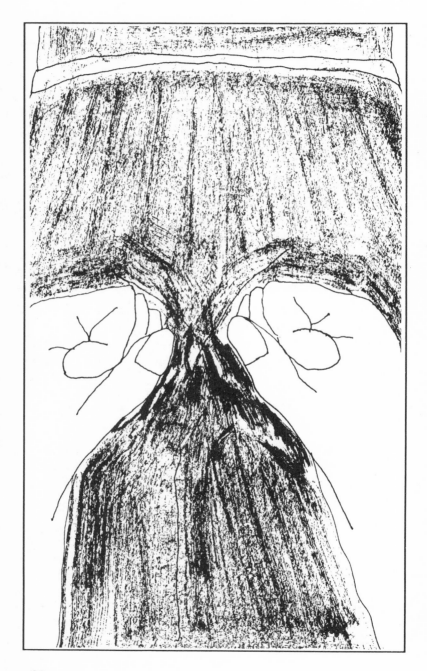

TOUCH

Mark 5:25-34: There was a woman in the area who had been af-
flicted with a hemorrhage for a dozen years.

She might just as well have been dead all those years as far as she was concerned. Cynthia had been hemorrhaging for twelve years. Hemorrhaging means bleeding, bleeding from the uterus. But it meant so much more than that. She was considered ritually unclean and therefore untouchable. Although the hemorrhaging occurred in only one part of her body, people reacted to her as though she herself were nothing but her hemorrhage. People kept her at arm's length. "Cynthia, keep your distance," was always the message, sometimes spoken, more often unspoken. Nobody would come close, not her family, not her relatives, not her friends. Only the physicians ever came close to her, but they touched her only if they had gloves to wear. Touch probably isn't the right word; probe and poke are more accurate.

"What does this feel like? Let me press here! We'd like to do a little probing there if you don't mind. When I squeeze, does it hurt?" On and on they went. But what hurt more than anything was the fact that while they were squeezing and pressing this part of her body and that part of her body, they never really touched her. She, Cynthia, was excluded from

Touch

their awareness while her body was studied and charted like some mysterious "thing." She was totally excluded from their awareness until it was time to send the bill. "Cynthia, this is the fee for our services. You can pay us now or you can pay us later, as long as you pay by the end of the month. Good bye, Cynthia."

At first she managed these bills with little trouble. She wasn't a wealthy woman, but she had some money, for a while. "For a while" because the first doctor's treatment failed to help her, then the second doctor's treatment failed, and so on. After twelve years and twice as many doctors, she was deeply in debt.

It would have been bad enough had it just been a matter of her spending all that money and not getting any better. What made it worse was the fact that she was a much sicker woman now. Had the disease actually gotten worse? Maybe and maybe not. But she felt worse. Her doctors continued to probe and poke but not with gloved hands. They used long, steel instruments that resembled artificial claws—cold to the touch and frightening to see. Every now and then a doctor might accidentally brush up against her. Horrified, he would immediately scour himself as if scrubbing some floor that hadn't been cleaned in years. Incidents like these made Cynthia feel even dirtier. She arrived at the point where she would warn them if she thought they were likely to touch her by accident. She came to see herself as they saw her. She looked upon herself as dirty, and she took it for granted she would never be touched. She had no right to be.

Not surprisingly, the desire to touch and be touched by another began to grow in her with a persistence that caused her as much pain as her hemorrhaging. But the more she wanted to touch and be touched, the more forcefully she was reminded of how untouchworthy she was. The tension was greatest the day she found herself caught up among a crowd of people. Ordinarily, she avoided crowds because she was so fearful of polluting them. On this particular day, however, she had taken the wrong turn home and within seconds found herself jostled along with the crowd.

She had no idea what was happening until she heard several people exclaim, "Jesus is here! Jesus is here!" She suddenly realized that not more than a few feet away from her stood the popular rabbi. She had heard of Jesus and of the power of his healing touch. In an instant, she knew she must touch him. Perhaps that could heal her! She would not presume to ask him to touch her. She was fearful that he would recognize her "uncleanness" and be repulsed. Yet, if she could just touch him—not even him, just some part of his clothing. Surely, this would be all right, and maybe, just maybe...

She inched toward him. She crouched on the ground a couple of feet away, hoping to remain unseen. She reached through the forest of legs that separated her from him to touch just the tassel of his cloak. Then it happened. Waves of relief and joy moved through her body. She couldn't believe it. She knew she had been cured! But suddenly a stern voice thundered, "Who touched me?" She froze where she was and a fear came over her. Jesus' disciples were taken aback. Everybody had been pressing in on him and touching him. What could they say except that everybody had touched him? But Cynthia knew Jesus had someone particular in mind. It had not been just another body that had touched him, but a person. And unlike the other healers, Jesus wasn't interested in healing only bodies; it was the hurting person aching to be touched that he wanted to touch and to heal.

Cynthia held back for as long as she dared. Trembling all over she stepped forward and the crowd gasped. But Jesus looked at her lovingly. He took her hand in his, put his arm around her shoulders and drew her near. Then he kissed her on the forehead as he said, "Daughter, it is your faith that has cured you. Go in peace and be free of this illness." Cynthia felt the warmth of his hand holding hers, the tenderness of his arm around her shoulder, and the gentleness of his kiss upon her forehead. It was as though a burden had been lifted. She felt good and clean and whole. He squeezed her hand and let her go as she cherished being touched, really touched, for the first time in years.

Reflection: Skin Hunger

We use the word "touch" to signify various kinds of intimacy and behavior. We want to "get in touch" with someone or we feel the need to "stay in touch." We are "touched" by a kind word or deed, and we are "touchy" about certain topics. Someone who is vulnerable is a "soft touch," while a person who knows exactly what is needed in a particular situation has the "right touch." And some people add "a touch of class" to whatever they do.

However varied the usage of the word, one thing is certain: touching and being touched are necessary for our well-being. Babies and children need to be touched by their parents, particularly by their mothers, in a way that communicates the parents' warmth and affection. The British psychiatrist W. D. Winnicott speaks of the holding environment for the child. He refers literally and metaphorically to the child's environment, wherein the mother holds or contains the child to communicate security. Children who are deprived of touch can suffer severe psychological problems.

But the need to touch and be touched doesn't stop when the child grows up, despite the fact that many people ignore that need once they reach adulthood. Interestingly, they develop what one observer has called skin hunger: a deep yearning for the touch that affirms, connects, assures, warms, and simply makes one feel, "I belong." However, because of fears associated with touching and how that might be interpreted, touching is severely limited or disguised as when men slap one another on the back or when male athletes slap one another's posterior.

Cynthia is never touched. The doctors probe and poke but that is not the right touch, not the human touch. She is made to feel like an object, not a subject. Her attitude toward herself grows to approximate the others' attitude towards her. She comes to consider herself untouchworthy, a condition not altogether unknown by many people today among whom are the elderly, the handicapped, and people with AIDS. Yet, her physical condition does not diminish her deep psychological need to touch and be touched. It intensifies it.

When there are no normal avenues of satisfying a pressing need, other ways will be found: "safe" ways. A voyeur "touches" another at a safe distance with his eyes, while others touch children. Even those whom we would consider normal might end up going to bed with veritable strangers, thinking that they wanted sex when what they really wanted was simply the warm touch and reassuring presence of another person. In all these cases, it might well be the lack of psychological and physical intimacy with their peers that sparks this kind of desperate behavior.

Cynthia wishes to touch Jesus secretly. She wants to be healed, but she wants to touch Jesus as an object in the same way she has been touched through the years. It is the healing power and not the healing person that she wants. Jesus will have none of this. He wants to know the person who seeks to be healed. His touch is not like those physicians' whose presence is absent when they touch. No, his touch is the touch of one person for another person.

Cynthia is healed by Jesus through his touch. How simple the lesson, this lesson in touching. How simple and yet how rare these days to find a healer who has the right touch.

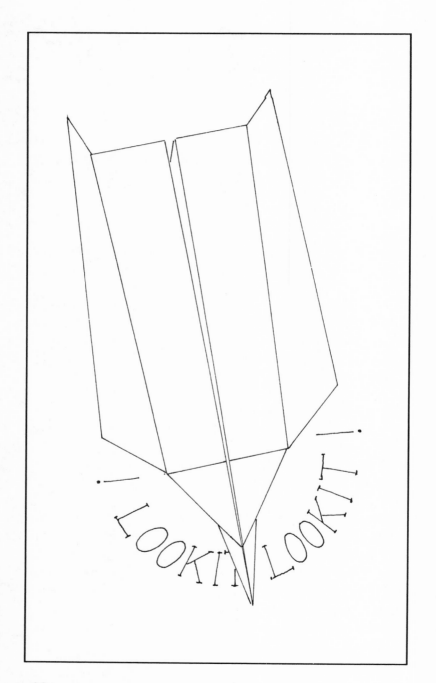

Years I and II: Monday of the 7th Week

NOTICING

Mark 9:14-29: "Teacher," a man in the crowd replied, "I have brought my son to you because he is possessed by a mute spirit."

"Look, mom!" but mom never did. "Look, dad!" but dad never did. It wasn't that what Aaron did was spectacular to look at. Nothing Aaron ever did was spectacular. He would make a little airplane out of paper as many other six years olds did. So, why bother to get excited about a paper airplane? Aaron liked to use his crayons to draw a yellow sun on a piece of paper and parade it around the house looking for "oohs" and "ahhs" from his mom and dad. Well mom and dad couldn't get excited about crayon marks on paper. They weren't about to go "ooh" and "ahh" over nothing. No, they'd be willing to grunt an occasional "oh, yeh" and an "I'm busy now," when they simply didn't want to be bothered at all.

Aaron felt he just wasn't trying hard enough. Maybe if he didn't eat all his food at the table, that would do it. Maybe mom and dad would notice then. Well mom and dad didn't notice. They'd talk about the weather; they'd talk about the neighbor's deaf dog; they'd coo about everything under the sun, except Aaron's crayon sun, that is. They simply never noticed that Aaron wasn't eating his food. Indeed, meal time was the time to see over, around, and under Aaron but never the time to see Aaron. Was any time the time to see Aaron?

Of course, Aaron knew mom and dad didn't see him because he just wasn't trying hard enough. It wasn't their fault they didn't notice him. Not eating his food was hardly the kind of act that would get mom and dad to notice him. So Aaron scratched his head, then scratched his head some more. When he scratched real hard, he saw little flakes of skin on his fingernails. Then he scratched all the more, not only his head but his arms and legs as well. Scratch, scratch, scratch! Aaron winced as he scratched, and his eyes opened wide as he scratched the little red marks on his arms into big red marks.

"Look, mom! Look, dad! Look at my arms! See the red marks, mom? See the red marks, dad?"

"Later!" Aaron's mom said as she closed her eyes and rocked away in her rocking chair.

"Later!" Aaron's dad said as he noticed the latest scores in the sports page.

"It's not their fault they don't see the red marks," Aaron thought. "How could they notice? My sweater is as red as the marks on my arm. That's why they didn't notice. If my sweater were blue, then they would have noticed!" And Aaron laughed so hard, he cried. Or did he cry so hard, he laughed? Really, did it matter at all since no one noticed anyway? So Aaron just stood and hit his head against the wall. At least the wall would notice he was there. Over and over again he hit his head against the wall.

"Stop making noise!" his mother said, her eyes still closed as she rocked away in her rocking chair."

"You're distracting me," dad said as he puffed on his pipe and noticed his team's standings.

"They hear me," Aaron said as he held his head in his hands. "They hear me," he said as he wiped the trickle of bloody sweat from his forehead. "Of course, they really shouldn't hear me or see me at all," Aaron added apologetically. "I've done nothing to be seen or heard." Then, slowly as saliva started gathering on his lips, "Silly me! Silly me!" he shouted and rolled his eyes till only the whites showed. "Silly me!" he screamed as his whole body opened and closed like a jack knife. "Silly me!" he raged as he fell to the ground wriggling on the floor like some speared snake. Someone or something had taken over Aaron and he had no control of himself.

And mom and dad? Surprise! They came running to Aaron and noticed him. Was this their son, they wondered? They weren't certain. It was hard to tell since they had hardly noticed him before. And why should they have noticed? What had he ever done before? But now. Well, now it was a different matter. What a spectacle! What a sight!

From that day on, Aaron's mom and dad noticed him. The attention they paid Aaron now equaled their earlier lack of attention. But Aaron too had changed. He ceased to speak and seemed unable to hear. And often there were violent seizures. Since they could never predict when the alien power would take over and send him into convulsions, his parents paid the closest attention to him during the years that followed. Slowly they began to appreciate the son they had never really noticed before.

Aaron's father wondered why his son experienced so much suffering. What had Aaron done to deserve this? His father even entertained the possibility that he and his wife might have had something to do with Aaron's suffering. It was just such a possibility that his father was considering one day as he led Aaron by the hand to the place where he had been told he could find Jesus of Nazareth. He knew Jesus was very busy, but he desperately wanted his son to be helped and he had heard about Jesus' healing powers. When he finally arrived, there was already a large crowd of people.

He was discouraged. Not only did he not see Jesus, but he didn't even know how he'd get Jesus to notice him and his son. He didn't have much time to consider what he would do next, however, because the jerky movements of Aaron's hand in his could mean only one thing: the alien power was at work in Aaron's body again.

Within seconds his son was in the familiar convulsive pattern. The crowd drew back and stared as Aaron twisted and turned on the ground. Then, two men came forward and gently laid their hands on Aaron as if to help him. But Aaron could not be quieted and his father felt helpless and distraught. Then looking up he saw another's hand stroke Aaron's head. He didn't need anyone to tell him what the crowd was now whispering among themselves. This was Jesus. Jesus had noticed his son. It was Jesus' hand on Aaron's head.

He questioned Aaron's father. "How long has this been happening to him?"

"From childhood," his father replied. "Often it throws him into fire and into water. You would think it would kill him. If out of the kindness of your heart you can do anything to help us, please do!"

Jesus said, " 'If I can'? Everything is possible to a man who notices."

The boy's father immediately exclaimed, "I do notice! Help me where I do not!"

Jesus, on seeing a crowd rapidly gathering, reprimanded the unclean spirit by saying to him, "Mute and deaf spirit, I command you: Get out of him and never enter him again!" Shouting and throwing Aaron into convulsions, it came out of him and Aaron became like a corpse, which caused many to say, "He is dead." But Jesus took him by the hand and helped him to his feet. "Aaron," Jesus said. "The alien power has left your body. You are safe. What is more, you don't need to worry any longer. They notice. They see you. They have learned to look after you." Having said these words, Jesus returned Aaron's hand into his father's, smiled, and left with his disciples.

And a smile came across Aaron's face that his father had never noticed before.

Reflection: Please Look

One explanation for why people are addicted to drugs or alcohol or food, etc., is that the addiction is a stimulus by means of which addicts know they are alive. An emptiness at the center of life is relieved, albeit temporarily, by the stimulus or kick that reminds them that they do exist. But the question this explanation raises is, what is the reason anyone might feel that he or she didn't exist? The story of Aaron may be able to answer that question.

Aaron wants to be noticed. Won't someone pay attention? He doesn't demand always being noticed, but he does want to be noticed some of the time. However, his parents don't have time to notice Aaron, although they do have the time to notice things like gardens and people like athletes. After a while he takes drastic measures to be noticed, measures that assure him he exists. He hits his head against the wall. At least the wall knows he is there and, with that reminder that he is there, Aaron is assured that he exists.

A modified version of self-inflicted pain to test reality is pinching ourselves and asking "Am I dreaming or is this for real?" There are other less drastic ways of determining one's identity or the continuity of one's identity in time. Elderly people may need to talk about their pasts over and over to anyone who will listen, hoping to glimpse in the other's response an assurance of their own being. A bag lady was observed at five in the morning standing in a telephone booth on Madison Avenue. She was talking loudly into the phone, reminding her non-existent partner at the other end of the line that she was John D. Rockefeller's daughter. It was a pathetic attempt on her part to be noticed and acknowledged by someone, even if that someone were a figment of her imagination. What Aaron did to be noticed is probably what we all might have done given his circumstances. We all want and need to know that we are.

But Aaron isn't noticed until he goes berserk. Then his parents notice. His parents' healing begins when they begin to notice. Is he really *their* son? What silly people! Why should it be difficult to recognize their own son? No more difficult than for relatives to recognize their own uncle or aunt who committed suicide, because *their* uncles and aunts don't do that kind of thing! No more difficult than for a married couple after 25 years looking at one another in their bed and saying "You aren't the person I married. Who are you?" When we begin to notice what we had not noticed, we notice just how different people have become.

Aaron's father notices, but he wants to be healed of his inability to notice, and that is what Jesus' healing is about. It is noticing that brings Aaron back. It is noticing that brings us all back and gives us the feeling that we really and truly exist. Noticing is indeed healing, the kind of healing that is needed if we really don't want people to take drastic measures in order to find out if they exist or not.

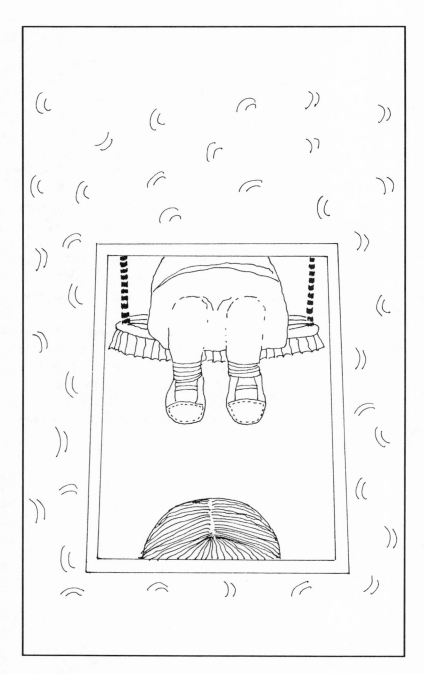

Cycle B: 7th Sunday in Ordinary Time
Years I and II: Friday of the 1st Week

CHUTZPAH

Mark 2:1-12: The four who carried him were unable to bring him to Jesus because of the crowd, so they began to open up the roof over the spot where Jesus was. When they had made a hole, they let down the mat on which the paralytic was lying.

Ben's friends remembered the good old days. Four of them gathered outside his bedroom one summer day. "I remember the time he sold sardine sandwiches to people who had been waiting in line hours for a job interview. Twenty minutes later he came by selling lemon-scented towelettes so they could clean their hands," one of his friends recounted.

Another friend joined in. "And there was the time he set up a roadblock and charged admission to the curious who wanted to see his neighbors' routine Friday night brawl on their front porch."

"You have to admit," a third friend added, "that he really outdid himself the time he freed his friend from jail. The Romans had no right to do what they did and Ben knew it. So he managed to sneak milk of magnesia into the jailer's scalloped potatoes and while the jailer was running back and forth, Ben slipped into the jail and got his friend out."

"Yes, Ben really fooled the Romans," a fourth friend chimed in, "but he also showed up the tax collectors. You can't deny he was at his best when he convinced them that his ring was worth five times as much as the money they said he owed them. They thought they had the better deal as they walked off with a trinket he had gotten from a box of Cracker Jacks."

"Yes, but remember when he convinced the guy who mugged him to loan him some money for a trip he said he had to take to visit his sick mother."

"And when you can convince your daughter that the D's she got on her report card stand for "diligent" and not "dumb" so that she tries ten times harder to improve, you really do have chutzpah," the third friend recalled.

They all laughed as they thought about Ben and the chutzpah he had shown throughout his life. Although Ben was still alive, he might as well have been dead. After his wife died two years ago, Ben had lain down on his mat and refused to get up. He told everybody he couldn't get up, that he was paralyzed. Many people believed Ben, no doubt, because he himself seemed so convinced he couldn't walk. However, some of his friends wouldn't buy it. No, they were convinced that Ben could walk again if he were sufficiently motivated. So they had met outside of Ben's home to discuss what they might do to help him.

Then one of them said, "You all probably know that Jesus of Nazareth is in town. He has cured a lot of people. If we could get Ben over there..."

"But how?" another interrupted.

"Suppose we tell him we'd like to carry him outside on his mat for a little exercise. Once we get him outside, we'll ask him if he'd mind our taking him to visit a friend who is seriously ill. If he doesn't object, we can get him to the place where Jesus is. The problem," the friend raised his finger "is how to get him in to see Jesus since I understand the crowds are so great it is impossible to get in the door."

"Well, that's where Ben is going to have to help us help him," a friend winked. "If chutzpah is what he had going for him, then maybe it'll be chutzpah that will help bring him back." They all agreed that that was where Ben's chutzpah would have to work for him.

When Ben's friends suggested taking him out for a little fresh air, he made no objection. "Go ahead," he said. "I'll never get any fresh air otherwise." Once they got him outside, they asked him if he would mind going with them to visit a very sick friend. Again, he had no objection. "Might as well," he muttered. "Nothing else I can do. I might as well go along." Their plan was working.

When Ben's friends neared the house where Jesus was, one of them said, "I don't know how we can possibly get in to see our friend. Just look at that crowd lined up to see him." Ben seemed surprised that so many people had chosen that particular afternoon to visit, but his friends could see by the look in his eyes that Ben was already dreaming up a way to get into the house.

"Do you have any idea how we can get in, Ben?" one of his friends asked.

"Hmmmm. Let me think." Ben had actually already come up with an idea, but it was a sign of his own chutzpah to keep his friends in suspense. "Knock on the door of the sick man's neighbor. Tell him we're tile inspectors who have come to look at the sick man's roof. Unfortunately, we left our ladder back at the office and we wonder if he could lend us one. Tell him if he lets us use the ladder, we'd be happy to inspect his own roof at half cost next week." Ben's friends agreed it was a good idea, and they were relieved to find Ben's chutzpah was still very much alive. Needless to say, the neighbor was delighted that the tile inspectors would inspect his roof for half price, and he gladly lent them his ladder.

Since Ben had thought up the scheme, he insisted on being part of carrying it out. "Just lift me up on my mat as you go up the ladder," he told his friends. Well, after a lot of effort, the four friends managed to get him up to the roof. What Ben didn't realize was that as two of his friends pulled him up and two pushed from behind, he was pushing and pulling himself, steadying himself with hands and feet on the rungs of the ladder. He hadn't moved that much in months! Perched atop the roof, they rested a moment as Ben congratulated them on hauling him up, still unaware of how much he had done.

After they had caught their breath, Ben pointed to the tiles on the center of the roof. "Remove those four center tiles that are resting on the frame," he told the others. Once they had removed the tiles, they all peered inside. What they saw was the young man Jesus directly below them on the ground level. A sprinkling of loose dirt from the loosened tiles had fallen on his head. Jesus looked up at them. Others in the room simply looked at one another in disbelief—but that was nothing new. They always looked in disbelief at anything and anyone, especially Jesus!

Ben didn't know what to make of it. "Where is the sick friend?" he wondered. But it isn't good chutzpah to let on when something doesn't seem quite kosher. So, he simply yelled down "Tile Inspectors! We have to come down and check the roof tiles from the ground level!" Awed by Ben's confidence, his friends lowered their ladder into the room. It was a little easier coming down than it had been going up; but even so, Ben had to work his hands and feet to steady himself on the ladder as they lowered him down.

Once on the ground Jesus looked at Ben and Ben looked at Jesus. There was instant rapport. Jesus smiled from ear to ear. His smile burst into the laughter of someone who could really appreciate chutzpah. Then Jesus looked at Ben's friends and shook his head in admiration. When he faced Ben again, it was with a look of compassion. Jesus knew how self-destructive people can be when they have lost hope or when they think they can do nothing and can in fact do a lot. Jesus said "Your sins are forgiven you!" Well, the ones who always looked in disbelief were really upset and carried on as if they would go through the roof. Ben knew about these men, these little men who had no compassion and what was even worse, no chutzpah! He wished he could teach them a lesson or two. No sooner had he thought this than his chance came.

The young man looked at Ben with a knowing look, the look of one who also had chutzpah. And between two people with chutzpah, nothing is impossible. Jesus said to Ben, "Stand up, pick up your mat, and go home."

Ben's eyes opened wide. "Not only is he asking me to get up but I have to haul my bed with me. He is something else! I'll go along with it. I'll pretend that I'm well enough to pick up my mat and walk straight out the door. That will show those naysayers!" With that Ben got up, picked up his mat, and left the house. Once outside, it dawned on him. Even he was taken in by what had happened. For here he was actually walking—he wasn't pretending, he was walking. Then he thought of that man Jesus, his smile, his knowing look, his compassion, his words.

Ben laughed, and slapped both knees with his hands. Then as he marched home with his mat, he let out a yell, "Now that's chutzpah!"

Reflection: Saving Grace

There are times in all our lives when we may be sorely tempted to throw in the towel. Someone close to us dies, as happened to Ben, or we see we are never going to accomplish all that we had hoped in our professions or places of work. Maybe we are just tired and we don't know why. We get depressed or disheartened and don't care what happens. We don't believe in ourselves anymore. Is there any hope? Perhaps, if there are friends around, real friends.

When friends have faith in us and in our abilities, then there is a possibility for a new lease. Friends are often able to emphasize and capitalize on some feature or characteristic we possess but have lost sight of as we drift depressed and without motivation. What endeared us to them in the first place may be the key to healing us of our paralysis and bringing us back into the land of the living. It might be our discarded sense of humor or compassion or gentleness that they seize upon to get us going again. Always, of course, it is their love for us that somehow has to get through to us. One man who had been severely depressed underwent psychiatric and drug treatment for his depression. When asked what he considered responsible for the dissipation of his depression, he said that he finally realized just how many people loved him and cared for him.

Ben's forgotten gift is his chutzpah. And his friends believe that if anything can bring Ben back, it is that chutzpah. And they are right. When Ben begins drawing on that reserve, his healing had already begun. Anyone who is depressed but can begin to imagine or project the self into a constructive situation is on the mend. Ben's mind and heart are engaged in finding a way to get into the house, and so his imagination draws him forward to such an extent that as his friends haul him up the ladder, he is already physically assisting them in his own recovery. And this physical and psychological healing continue as he lets his chutzpah draw him down into the house where Jesus stands.

The matching of Jesus' chutzpah with Ben's is a confirmation that Ben's friends were on the right track. Jesus heals Ben by capitalizing and affirming what is so lovable about him. He does so by modeling Ben's own chutzpah in the context of compassion. Jesus is compassionate chutzpah at work, and it is that which brings Ben's healing to completion as he picks up his mat and, to his own surprise, finds that he is healed. Still, the communal nature of this healing is emphasized when Jesus refers to Ben's friends who believe in him. Ben is choked up with emotion because he realizes, as we all do, that when we give up on ourselves, every now and then there are people in our lives who are there to say, "You can do it. Get up and walk. We're with you." And we get up and walk.

Cycle C: 28th Sunday in Ordinary Time
Year I: Wednesday of the 32nd Week
Thanksgiving Day

THANK YOU

Luke 17:11-19: One of them, realizing that he had been cured, came back praising God in a loud voice. He threw himself on his face at the feet of Jesus and spoke his praises. This man was a Samaritan.

They were flirting with danger. Jesus and a handful of his disciples weren't always certain whether they were in Galilee or Samaria. They had started out on their way to Jerusalem with the intention of walking on the Galilee border side, but the path they took seemed to twist and turn in such a way that in the absence of markers it was difficult to tell just where they were. Since it was a very hot day, they decided to rest for two or three hours before continuing their journey. They stopped near a stream, took off their knapsacks, sat down, and plunged their feet into the cool water as it gently flowed along.

They hadn't been there more than thirty minutes when they heard a rustling sound in a clump of trees less than fifty feet away. Philip, who had been dozing off, blinked his eyes, looked in the direction of the noise, and quickly alerted the others. "Jesus! Pete! Jim! Look over there," he whispered. And coming out of the clump of trees were seven, eight, nine men, no, ten, for the last one didn't emerge until all of the others were considerably ahead of him.

"Lepers!" James whispered as he pulled his feet out of the stream and put on his sandals. The nine lepers and the tenth one, who was still a few steps away from the others, were moving toward Jesus and his disciples. Philip and Peter yanked their feet from the stream and, without waiting to put on their sandals, stood up and began to retreat from the advancing lepers. Jesus ordered them to stop.

"What is wrong with you? How long have you been with me? Are you still afraid? Have you still so little love?" His voice betrayed both anger and disappointment. Then, more gently he said, "It's all right. I will go to them." Jesus slowly lifted his own feet out of the water, put on his sandals, got up, and walked over to the lepers.

"How are you today? Have you had anything to eat? Perhaps we could share some of our wine with you. We have a couple of cups and could all take turns using them." He could hear Peter, James, and Philip all groaning at the idea of everybody sharing the same cups. As if to dispel their fears, he added "Of course, if you have a cup, I would be happy to pour the wine into that cup and you could all share from it." Since Jesus heard no further groans, he guessed that the small crisis had passed.

One of the lepers moved a bit closer to Jesus, but not too close since the leper was so accustomed to people backing off when he or any of the others crossed some invisible line. "Jesus, we need your help. Can you help us?"

"What is your name? I would like to know your name." Jesus seemed genuinely interested.

"My name?" The leper was surprised. It had been so long since anyone had asked him his name, he was taken aback by the question. "Why, my name is Dan," he said.

"Thank you, Dan. I always like to know who I'm talking to. Now what can I do for you, Dan?"

"Well, as you can see, all of us are in pretty bad shape and we were wondering, could you..." he hesitated. "Could you in any way help us? I mean, could you cure us?"

Jesus smiled. "I think that would be possible. But I would like to know who the others are before I do anything."

"You would?" Dan said with growing surprise.

"Yes. It's always a pleasure for me to get to know the people who come to me."

Dan nodded approvingly and then turned to the others. One by one they came forward as Dan introduced them. Jesus took each one by the hand and held it for a minute as he asked where each was from, how old each was, what each had hoped to do in life before the leprosy had appeared. Obviously, he was moved by what some of them had to say, since tears welled up in his eyes from time to time. Finally, Dan turned expectantly to Jesus and announced that now he had introduced all of them. Jesus was about to thank them all for talking with him when he caught sight of the one who had trailed behind the others when they had emerged from the trees, the one who never walked along with the rest.

"And who is that man?" Jesus asked as he pointed in the direction of the leper standing at a distance.

"Him?" Dan didn't even seem to see him. "Oh, he's a Samaritan."

"Yes, but what is his name?" Jesus appeared unconcerned to find a Samaritan in Jewish company.

"His name?" Dan was embarrassed. "I don't know."

"You don't know?" Jesus had a touch of anger in his voice. "Call him over. Better yet, I will go to him." Jesus walked over to the Samaritan. "And what is your name?"

If Dan had been surprised when Jesus asked him his name, this tenth man was dumbfounded. "My name is Jonathan, yes, Jonathan," he said as if he himself were no longer certain.

"Can I call you, Jon, for short?"

Jonathan seemed stunned and then pleased. "Jon? Why yes, of course. I used to be called Jon by my friends—when I had friends." The last couple of words were followed by silence, a silence that bonded Jesus to this man immediately.

"Has anybody ever told you, Jon, that you have very honest-looking eyes?" Jesus said as he carefully studied Jonathan's face.

Jonathan's eyes opened wide and a smile came across his face. "No, sir, no one has ever told me that."

"Well, you do and it's worth saying 'Amen' about." Jesus then put his arm around Jonathan and said, "Amen," to which Jonathan answered, "Amen" as he put his own arm around Jesus' waist. With his gentle arm around Jonathan's shoulders, he turned to the others and told them, "I want you to go to the priests. They will attest to the fact that you no longer have leprosy." The lepers looked at one another. They didn't know what to say. They would say nothing until they had gone to the priest, since nothing seemed to have happened to them thus far. More in obedience than in hope, they all turned and quietly left Jesus. Jonathan smiled at Jesus as he too left, trailing the others who didn't appear to notice him at all.

Then Jesus and his disciples sat down at the stream once again and this time fell asleep for a couple of hours. When they awoke, the disciples saw to their surprise that Jonathan was back, standing at a distance talking quietly to Jesus.

"But what happened to Dan and the others?" Jesus asked with obvious disappointment. He had taken time with them, talked with them, and healed them. And then they vanished without one word of thanks. "Sometimes I feel like I'm just being used," Jesus said. "They want me to heal them and I want to. But I must say that sometimes I feel like a 'thing' that is forgotten as soon as the job is done."

"There now." It was Jonathan's turn to comfort Jesus. "I would have liked you as a friend whether you had healed me or not. After all, nobody had called me Jon in years. You were the first one, and that meant a lot to me. I'm grateful to God for all you have done. Certainly, I'm grateful for the healing, but even more for making me feel human again even while I was a leper." There was a moment of silence between them and then Jonathan continued, "By the way, did anybody ever tell you that you have a very infectious smile?"

Jesus looked at Jonathan with surprise and delight. "Really?"

"Really!" Jonathan smiled back.

"Well, thank you, Jon. Thank you. You've made my day!" And the two of them walked arm in arm back to the disciples to share a cup of wine.

Reflection:
Taken For Granted

It is possible to think of relating to ourselves and others in two ways: being taken for granted and taking for granted. To be taken for granted feels like being used as a thing for the benefit of another person. It's like being a drinking fountain, a mere convenience. On the other hand, to take for granted means that it goes without saying that a person or thing always ought to be there for us. When we take people for granted, we become leprous because our senses are progressively deadened.

We no longer see, touch, hear, or taste the realities we take for granted. A man comes to the table for breakfast and as he eats he reads the morning paper. His wife is there and his children as well, but he does not see them. He may nod his head in their direction, thereby signaling that he is dimly aware of their presence, but that is not really seeing or acknowledging their presence. They could be doing handstands or plotting his death and he wouldn't know the difference. As he eats his breakfast he is oblivious to the texture and taste of his food. He takes his food for granted as well as his family. There is a fresh bouquet of carnations on the table, but he doesn't really see them. They too are taken for granted. His senses are deadened to what there is to see, hear, feel, and taste. This is why taking for granted is leprous.

Jesus doesn't take any of the lepers for granted in this story. They are not just a new batch of lepers with the same old problem in need of the same old cure. Jesus does not crank out healing miracles like some dispensing machine. He wants to know each of them by name. They aren't just lepers. They are individuals with unique personalities. So he is taken aback when one of the lepers doesn't even realize he hasn't introduced Jesus to the Samaritan.

Since Jesus doesn't take people for granted, it is understandable that he himself resents being taken for granted. This is not a sign of immaturity so much as it is a protest against being made into a mere convenience. It is the healed Samaritan who now ministers to Jesus in his taken-for-grantedness, and he does so as any healed leper should. He really sees, hears, and touches the pain of Jesus in his taken-for-grantedness and in so doing mirrors back to Jesus—Jesus the person and not Jesus the thing. This mirroring response is also the gracious response of one who has been saved from being taken for granted.

"Thank You" is the alert, attentive response of those who take no person or thing for granted but regard all who enter their lives as gifts, sheer gifts.

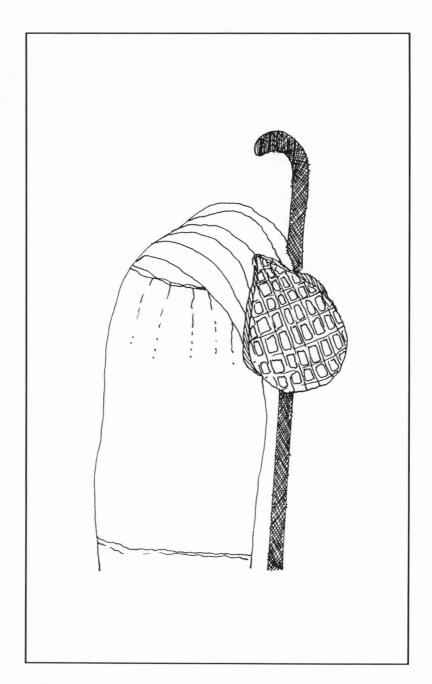

FEET

Luke 13:10-17: There was a woman there who for eighteen years had been possessed by a spirit which drained her strength. She was badly stooped — quite incapable of standing erect.

I just wonder how many people have seen as much of the world as I have. I bet there are very few." Alice chuckled to herself as she scanned the ground on her way to the synagogue. She chuckled because all of what she had seen of the world was pretty much what she was looking at right now and had looked at for the past eighteen years. She was so stooped that she could no longer look into persons' faces when they talked. To see it, she would ask the person to stand about ten feet away. From that distance, she could see; however, since she also had poor hearing, she had to choose between hearing the person up close or seeing the person at a distance. Frequently, she settled for a compromise. She'd listen to the person up close and then ask them to stand ten feet away for the last few minutes of their conversation.

She'd laugh and tell her visitors, "You can't have both at the same time and that's OK. It's either your face or your voice that gets all my attention. Plus then it's easier to tell whether they're pulling a fast one on me or not." She felt she was lucky because when the conversation was boring, she could close her eyes and her guests or her host would never know the difference. "I can even yawn and make faces as much as I want. You see how much freedom I have to be myself? And feet? How many people have seen as many feet as I have? I'm not bragging, but if you are interested in statistics, you could say I come across twice as many feet as I do faces in a day's time."

Of course, Alice spent little time talking about the constant pain she suffered. She would never complain about how her back ached day and night. Nor would she dwell on the fact that so many people completely ignored her. They would always see over her or around her but seldom saw her. And since it was as difficult for them to see her face as for her to see theirs, the expression "out of sight, out of mind" had a special application when it came to Alice.

That spring morning Alice made her way to the synagogue as she had every day for the past ten years. She navigated through the busy traffic, crossing streets only when she saw the other feet alongside of hers doing the same. She couldn't keep up with them but she could start out with them and she was grateful for that.

Because she didn't see the others' faces and no one saw hers, she had a kind of invisibility that protected her from the street bullies who bothered other older people as they walked about the village.

When she finally arrived at the synagogue, she took her usual chair near the back. Since all she saw while sitting were her own feet, she decided it mattered little where she sat. And if she wanted different scenery, all she had to do was change the color of her socks. Because it was the Sabbath, there were quite a few others at the synagogue. Indeed, by her reckoning, there were an unusual number of feet that day.

She hadn't been sitting there more than fifteen minutes when she noticed two other feet pointed toe to toe with her own. That could only mean one thing: the person to whom these feet belonged was interested in her for some reason. No one there was ever interested in her except if it were time to collect some money for the poor. She reached in her pocket and pulled out a coin, which she extended to whomever was doing the collecting. She waited and waited.

"No, that isn't what I want, but thanks just the same." Then she felt a hand on her back. At first she was startled, but there was something very soothing about that hand, as there had been in the voice. It felt as if the warmth radiating from the hand spread over her whole back. Then she heard the voice say, "Woman you are free of your sickness."

Alice would have laughed out loud had it not been for that warmth that seemed to create an incredible flexibility in her neck and back. And she knew it was true when, to get a glimpse of this kind man's face, she found to her surprise that she was able to lift her head and look the man square in the eyes with no effort whatsoever. For the first time in years she was able to look someone in the face—and what a face! The man was smiling at her, reflecting the same wonder she herself was experiencing. He seemed equally overjoyed at what was happening.

"You look wonderful!" he told her. She was about to tell him how grateful she was not to have to look at feet again when a voice as cold as the young man's was warm echoed throughout the synagogue.

"There are six days for working. Come on one of those days to be cured, not on the Sabbath."

She knew the voice of the chief of the synagogue, and she wasn't afraid of him. "There's no warm blood in those veins! But I'll go to him and explain."

Jesus raised his hand. "No, I will take care of it. I've run into his kind before." Before she knew it, he was at the front of the synagogue. When he spoke, everyone straightened up and listened. He addressed the elders who were sitting with the chief of the synagogue. "You're real hypocrites. Tell me, which one of you doesn't let his ox or ass out of the stall on the Sabbath to water it? This woman has suffered for eighteen years. Don't you think she deserved to be healed as soon as possible, Sabbath or no Sabbath? When are you going to get some warm blood in those cold veins of yours?" He turned and winked at Alice, as the whole congregation burst into applause.

"Right on! It's about time someone let them have it! Thank God someone told them off!" Men, women, and children spoke up all over the congregation, much to the dismay of the chief of the congregation.

By the time Jesus had made his way back to Alice, she was applauding and even dancing a little jig. "You may not be able to stay in the same congregation after today," Jesus said with some concern.

"Oh, I'm not worried about that," Alice said with complete assurance. "Nothing and no one can take away my thanks to God for all that has happened today." And with a twinkle in her eyes, she said to Jesus, "Do you know you have a hole in your sandals? Come over to my place. No one knows shoes and sandals like I do." And together, heads held high, they both walked out of the synagogue and over to Alice's house.

Reflection: New Horizons

The most significant dimension of the healing that takes place in this story is not obvious. It isn't obvious because the physical nature of the healing is so striking. That is true of most of Jesus' miracles, but this should not prevent us from imagining what is taking place beneath those appearances. What more could possibly be taking place here besides the physical cure of a woman who has been so bent for so many years that she can only see people's feet? One answer to this question is she is cured of being simply a feet person.

We can speak of people in terms of their orientation as heads-in-the-cloud people or down-to-earth people: head people versus feet people. Head people are always looking upward. They are idealists and romantics who aspire to do great things in life. They are visionaries: they dream and imagine what can be. Anything is possible for the head people and we are grateful to them because they inspire us.

But head people have their problems too. They can't abide routine, humdrum, day in and day out routine. Moreover, they have a disregard for practical matters; they aren't pragmatic. They dream dreams, but they aren't sure how to carry them out. They can't be bothered by others who want a detailed, concrete blueprint regarding the implementation of the dream. They easily get carried away and lose touch with reality. They are deeply in need of the feet people.

Feet people are down to earth. They are grounded in the here and now, with fewer illusions about life and what it promises. If they ever had dreams, they were disillusioned through suffering. Life is not an enchanted forest for feet people. They are grateful for their food and for their home and for their children, if they have any or all three. Unlike head people, they don't get carried away, rooted as they are in the soil. They are "no nonsense" people, although they enjoy a good chuckle.

If there is a dark side to feet people, it is that they may end up having no vision, no expectations at all. They may turn sour and cynical as their horizons shrink to satisfying immediate bodily needs. Routine deepens into a rut, and they can live their lives oblivious to the spouse or friend in the next room or the next house.

Alice is a feet person. Every day she goes back and forth to the synagogue and to the grocery store. These trips absorb Alice's time and energy completely, leaving little time for anything else. To a head person, Alice's routine appears mind-numbingly dull, but as we have seen, Alice has a wisdom born and nurtured in her small world. She doesn't speak of visions as a head person does, but she has her own insights derived from years of being close to the earth.

Then Jesus comes on the scene and brings a change into her life. He heals her so she can straighten up and look upward and forward. What a change for a feet person. To be able to look up to the skies with their clouds and sun! For the first time she can reach up and be a head person. But this presents new opportunities and challenges for her. What will she do as she looks directly into others' faces? Smile or scowl? Be inviting or rejecting? We don't know.

Alice's healing, then, is much greater than a healing of her body. It is a healing that opens her up to new horizons. It is also the kind of healing that every feet person might want for himself or herself, whereas every head person might want the healing that opens to becoming a feet person. The healing that brings head and feet together is the healing Jesus tried to accomplish in Alice.

DREAMER

*Matthew 17:1-9: He was transfigured before their eyes. His face be-
came as dazzling as the sun, his clothes as radiant as light.*

Reuben's brothers and sisters kept telling him, "Reuben,
Reuben, you're so out of it! You're such a dreamer!"
Reuben's friends kept telling him, "This is the real world — get
with it!" He had heard it so many times. At first his parents
thought it was just a passing phase. But now Reuben was 28.
"This isn't a phase," his mother finally admitted. "This is a disease!"

What really upset them was when Reuben spent so much
time talking about when the Kingdom Day would arrive: how
everyone would sit around the Big One's table, laughing, telling jokes, eating bagels and lox, and making plans to enlarge
the table so more and more people could sit around it.
"Reuben, be practical," his brother said. "We can't earn a
living off your dreams. We've got to tend our flocks and mind
our business. When will you stop all this daydreaming?"

Of course, if all Reuben's family and friends had to contend
with was Reuben's daydreaming, that would have been one
thing. What fired them up the most was the company he kept.
Reuben spent time with what his family labeled the ne'er-do-

wells, the riffraff, the dips, the local yokels. He was forever sharing his dreams with them, one on one or sitting around a table. He talked with whoever wanted to talk.

"What does he think he's doing, spreading nonsense to these country bumpkins about some future happy hour in the sky? Why does he fill them with all these false hopes? Doesn't he know or understand that life is to be lived here and now?"

Of course they had a point, didn't they? Never mind that as he shared his dreams and whatever food and drink he brought with him, the "riffraff" felt like they were already starting to live what they were dreaming about. Never mind that Ruth the servant girl got the biggest kick out of dreaming about the day when she'd be rubbing elbows at the same table with Leah, her mistress. Never mind that Sol the half-wit smiled from ear to ear because for the first time someone, Reuben, cared enough to share something with him. Never mind that toothless Tara laughed as she had never laughed before! She imagined herself dressed to kill in an outfit that would raise the eyebrows of those who turned up their noses at her now. None of this seemed to mean anything to Reuben's family, if they even noticed it to begin with.

What finally made them put their collective foot down was Reuben's trips to the leper colony. Reuben took his dreams to the lepers. At first they, too, thought he was a little crazy, feeding them dreams about better days. Yet, gradually even the lepers began to change. They started showing more interest in their appearances because, as one of them put it, "We'd like to get a head start in preparing for the glory of the Kingdom Day." Lay their newfound self-esteem to Reuben's dreams or to Reuben's charm or both; the point is, they were changing. Instead of despair there was hope. For Reuben's family, however, teaching lepers to dream dreams was just so much useless activity. They gave Reuben the ultimatum,

"Go and think over what you have done. Then either stop your daydreaming and live as we do, or don't even come back to live with us."

Well, Reuben felt awful. What would he do? Maybe they were right. Maybe this daydreaming was alot of nonsense, just so much silliness. He wandered the countryside in a daze, determined once and for all to make up his mind about his future. As he neared one remote mountaintop, he thought he heard voices. He looked over in that direction and saw four men sitting on the ground. They had a jug of wine, a loaf of bread, and some cheese resting on a patch of green grass in front of them.

At first no one noticed Reuben because they were so caught up in their conversation. Then one of the men looked toward Reuben, smiled, and motioned with his hand for Reuben to come join them. Reuben hesitated, but the man's smile was so warm that it was irresistible. The young man introduced himself as Jesus, son of Joseph, and then turned and introduced his friends, Peter, James, and John. Reuben's eyes lit up. He had heard of this Jesus. Indeed, his parents often compared Reuben's useless daydreams to Jesus'.

Jesus invited Reuben to sit down and offered him some wine and bread. He went on to tell Reuben that the four of them were sharing their dreams about the future, about the day when all the children of the Holy One would be gathered around the table, when young and old alike would never cry again but would laugh and enjoy one another's company. Reuben couldn't believe what he was hearing. This Jesus was recounting Reuben's own dreams, putting into words Reuben's own hopes, singing the words of the song Reuben had sung alone for so long.

And as he listened, his eyes riveted to Jesus' face. He didn't know whether it was the bright sun, but even as he gazed at Jesus, he saw a radiance and a light that he had never seen before. Indeed, not just Jesus' face but his garments as well seemed to intensify the sun's light, and Reuben had to shield his eyes. He could hear Jesus' friend Peter cry out how good it was for them to be there. Reuben shook his head as though to wake up, for he could have sworn that there were now two more men who had not been there before, and they were talking with Jesus. Reuben felt deep inside that here was a man who must be very close to God. He looked up to see where the sun was and how it came to shine so brightly on Jesus. To his astonishment, Reuben could find no sun. The whole sky was overcast, but then where was the light coming from? When he looked back to Jesus, the intense light was gone and Jesus was sitting there simply smiling.

Reuben wondered whether he had been daydreaming again. Jesus set Reuben's mind at rest when he told all of them that they were not to tell anyone what they had seen. Reuben gave a sigh of relief! "No, I haven't been daydreaming. But then..." He hit his head lightly with the palm of his hand. "Of course, I have been daydreaming," he said to himself. "And it was a good thing I had dreamed dreams all along, or I'd never have been able to dream this dream on the mountaintop with Jesus and his friends." It was precisely because he had dreamed dreams all along that he could see something marvelous in Jesus that his family and friends would never see. Now he had the answer he was looking for. He would not stop dreaming his dreams, even if it meant leaving his home for good. His dreams were too precious.

Jesus looked at Reuben, smiled, and said, "Come, it is time to leave the mountaintop. What you were looking for, you have found."

Reflection: Can You Imagine?

"Stop your daydreaming. Pay attention." How many times have we heard someone tell us that? Certainly teachers in school and our work supervisors use that line over and over. Daydreaming along with fantasizing and imagining are regarded as useless activities. We are told to be realistic and to not get carried away by our dreams. Of course, later in life we end up going to psychiatrists, who tells us to let our minds roam and tell them our dreams. We end up paying someone else to undo what we were told not to do earlier in life.

The realm of the imagination is not a tourist attraction that our educators or religious leaders or authorities encourage us to visit. That is a pity. The imaginative realm is the arena in which we say, "Let's pretend; let's make believe." And in our pretending we are introduced to "as if" scenarios. For example, we pretend God is a mother and we talk to her "as if." Or we make believe God is an ocean and we picture ourselves swimming in God "as if." "But," someone will object, " 'as if' is not for real. After all, we all know God is father, not mother. And how can you make God an ocean when God is a person?" Our response to this objection is that the world of pretend is both for real and not for real. Is the character of Willy Loman in *Death of A Salesman* real when we see him walking about on the stage? The actor pretending to be Willy Loman is not Willy Loman, but he is not *not* Willy Loman either. And we who enter Willy's world, in our pretending to be there, are we there or aren't we? His world isn't our world, but at that moment it is not *not* our world either. Pretending draws us into a world that has its own reality, the reality of "as if." And in that "as if" world we are given a vision of what might be.

Visions are at home in the imaginative realm. When we have visions, we are imaginatively entering into the future or letting the future begin to transform the present. The vision initiates the future in the present moment. We could say it is the preview of coming attractions, but that is putting it too mildly. The reality of the coming attraction is already present in the vision and serves to guide and direct the visionary in the present. When children play pretend, they are already becoming socialized into the roles they "try on" in the backyard.

Reuben shared his dream with those less fortunate, and the sharing of the dream began initiating the Kingdom Day. Reuben, Jesus, and the others pretended, imagined, envisioned; the reign of God came into being because it shaped and molded those who imagined and dreamt. Reuben recognizes in Jesus a kindred dreamer, and it is on the mountaintop that only a dreamer could have appreciated the transfiguration. Literalists can only ask one thing. Did it really happen that way? We saw that Alice in "Feet" was cured not only of her physical illness; she was also healed from being simply a feet person. Alice could now dream dreams. The literalist also needs to be healed of his literalism. He or she needs to experience the kind of healing that will enable him or her to touch and be touched by the reign of God, which comes to those who can imagine and dream about it. Reuben didn't need to be healed of any literalism; he did need to be affirmed in the validity of his dream by the one who could make it all come true.

136

RAGE

Mark 5:1: "Legion is my name. There are hundreds of us."

He had enough rage in him to supply a whole legion of soldiers. Who would have guessed that this man with the terribly contorted face and body was just a year ago a sensitive, caring young man, or so it seemed. What had happened to him that brought about such a transformation?

Why, he had been sensitive and caring for as long as anyone could remember. Certainly, he had been sensitive to his mother's needs, especially since his father had run off with another woman. "The little man," as his mother put it, saw to it that she was proud of him as she had always wanted to be. Indeed, she had insisted on being proud of him!

He was neat and clean in appearance, not given to getting soiled or messy as the other boys were. Frequently, she made it a point to mention to the neighbors how happy she was when he was her neat, sparkling little man. And if there were times when he wasn't neat or clean? Well, she would never scold him, never! She might look a little sad but mostly she would play a little game with him, or better, a game on him. She would pretend he didn't exist. She just wouldn't notice him as he looked at her with fear in his eyes. She would see through him until he got the point and then she would just laugh. He did get the point, but not without getting some vague, nameless feeling that held some terror for him.

What she really liked and praised were his manners. He was so well mannered, and she loved to take him to restaurants and to her friends' homes to display him. "What a little man he is," she'd say. "Isn't he a little gentleman?" she'd ask. "Such a gentleman," she'd chortle to anyone in hearing distance. And of course, she knew how good he must have felt when she said this. Or so she thought.

Of course, if he slipped up and showed signs of being ill mannered—if he dropped his napkin or spilled his milk on his little tie—she'd just play a little game with him, or better, a game on him. She would pretend he didn't exist. She just wouldn't notice him as he looked at her with fear in his eyes. She would see through him until he got the point and then she would just laugh. And he did get the point, but not without some uneasiness that something inside of him was moving restlessly about, something too terrible to get close to.

It gave her considerable delight when he said he was going to school to become a lawyer. That was what she had encouraged him to be all along. What a surprise that he would choose to be a lawyer! Of course, she had told him right along that he had the talents to be a lawyer. Of course, she had also pointed out how well he could talk, how persuasively he could argue, and how he could use others. Use others? Did she say that? What she meant was how well he could be of use to others. How silly of her to make that kind of a mistake. She felt she had a hand in his decision, but she would be modest about it. In fact, she'd even make a little joke about it to her friends. "If he decided to do something else, well, I think I'd just pretend he didn't exist," she'd say and then she'd laugh.

He was such a good son, her little man. He knew how to please his mother. He knew how to win her affection. He felt so good when she smiled at him, and he made certain that she kept smiling. True, from time to time, when he missed the boat and she played the game that he didn't exist, he felt like nobody, an empty shell. And true, from time to time, when he missed the boat he felt the terror of that nameless force dancing on the edge of consciousness. But he was always able to become the good little man again.

One day the happy young lawyer felt drawn to a young woman that he met. He felt so deeply for her that it was just a matter of time before he wanted to bring her home to meet his mother. When she saw the girl, she smiled at the girl, looked at her son, and said, "You like her?"

"Yes, mother," he said.

"Well she's lovely. She's intelligent. She'll make someone a nice wife. As for you, do you remember the game we used to play?" At that moment the game she had played so often to keep him in line was over. He snapped, and the nameless feeling, the terrible feeling took over. He could not be restrained or contained. He raged and raged! It seemed as though a thousand devils were having their day at last. And their name was legion!

And they brought him to this place of death, this place among the tombs. There, day and night, he howled with rage that echoed and amplified the rage a thousandfold. Not only did he move about the tombs but he would beat his head against them, so uncontrollable was his rage against himself as well as others.

Then, on a particularly stormy morning, the pain-wracked man made his way to the lake shore close by to drown himself and end his life. There on the shore, however, stood a man who appeared to be waiting for him. What did he want, this man clothed in a simple white tunic? The man possessed felt his rage as he had never felt it before. Armed with this rage, he ran forward with arms outstretched to do battle with this stranger. Instead, he found himself on his knees with arms outstretched, pleading, "Why meddle with me, Jesus, Son of God Most High? I implore you in God's name, do not torture me." This he cried because he was aware that the one who stood before him was already engaged in the struggle for his soul.

"What is your name?" charged the man in white.

"Legion is my name," he answered. "There are hundreds of us." And then he vomited up his rage in abusive language on this man. Over and over again it came in waves but the man in white stood his ground and would not budge. The man possessed could not destroy the other with his rage, nor did the other play on him the game that the man possessed had experienced so often in the past. The other simply let him be and let him be in such a way that he came to feel he could be without playing any game at all.

Then, and only then, the raging stopped and in its place tears welled up in the man possessed as he drew near to Jesus and placed his head upon his lap. Now he felt like someone who had not ceased to be but like a new being who didn't need to play at being good because in Jesus' presence he had experienced beneath his rage the deep down goodness in himself. Finally, he was at peace as he sat there fully clothed and perfectly sane.

Reflection:
Last Straw

"I simply don't believe it. It's impossible. He couldn't have done it. He's so mild and caring." These and similar comments we often read in newspaper accounts of men or women who have murdered a spouse or parent. It is difficult to understand how a gentle, sensitive, caring person can commit an act of violence on a loved one. Or is it?

Many sensitive, caring people have learned to be that way at an early age as a matter of survival in the home. Alice Miller, in her book *Drama of the Gifted Child* (formerly titled *Prisoners of Childhood*), describes some of the parents of children who grow up to be professional caregivers. These parents regard the children as extensions of themselves. Their children exist for them. They learn how to respond to their parents' moods and expectations to ensure some kind of parental acceptance. But there is a price to pay for developing a sensitivity to their parents' feelings while ignoring their own feelings. Whatever hurt or resentment lies within is never owned or admitted. They can't receive their own feelings into consciousness because it would threaten their relationship with a parent.

The young man in "Rage" is portrayed as sensitive, and he probably is so for the same reasons Alice Miller gives in her book. Although he never acts violently toward his mother, he does reach a point where he can no longer contain his rage and he explodes. The next thing we know, he is possessed and living among the tombs.

But who is really possessed, the man or his mother? It is she who uses and abuses him. The real evil lies in her manipulating him at every turn. And what about his rage? Surely it is the result of anger contained too long—an anger directed against a person who continually violated him. Rage is his last defense, a defense all of us use from time to time when we sense we have been violated or shamed. We, too, reach our limits when we will have no more games played on us! And how long does the rage last?

The young man is not healed by words of advice from Jesus. Jesus doesn't preach or lecture or moralize or write him a prescription to calm his nerves. He simply is there for the man in a way his mother never was. There is no manipulation, no game playing; and once the man's rage has played itself out, he can experience deep within the goodness of his own being, which Jesus evokes through his own presence.

It is important to underline what takes place in Jesus' healing. The man experiences the goodness of his own being, not a goodness based on being good. The latter is precisely what his whole life was about previously, and the pressure his mother applied on him to be the compliant, good little boy resulted in his rage. Experiencing the goodness of his being was an altogether different experience, more like the experience of saying "I am" on a glorious spring day.

DAY OFF

Mark 7:24-29: Soon a woman, whose small daughter had an unclean spirit, heard about him. She approached him and crouched at his feet.

Everybody needs time off. Jesus was no exception. He had had a particularly busy week. There were an exceptional number of persons who needed his gentle touch and kind words. Why just yesterday he spent two hours consoling Mr. Schnitzel over the death of Mrs. Schnitzel.

After he had spent this time with Mr. Schnitzel, Miriam Moskevitz called him to say some prayers for her ninety-year-old father, who hadn't responded to her call to get out of bed in the morning. He had died, she thought. It was a false alarm. Mr. Moskevitz had played dead because he thought finally someone would pay attention to him. Jesus took him by the hand and together they sat, split a bottle of beer, and talked about some of the older Jewish ladies that had their eyes on Mr. Moskevitz. Mr. Moskevitz thought he would pay them a visit soon. The episode with Mr. Moskevitz took a couple of hours as did the time he spent with Mr. Schnitzel.

Then there were the usual number of persons who just wanted Jesus to touch them--people who had all kinds of aches and pains. He would touch them gently where they hurt as they pointed to those parts of their bodies where they experienced hurt. Since he always spent a little additional time chatting with each of them and never hurrying them, a good part of the day was used up in this activity.

So Jesus decided to take one day off and went to an area where he thought no one would recognize him. He even wore colored glasses that day and wore a robe with a hood that covered his head and partially covered his face. "I'm safe," he thought. "I feel a little guilty taking some time off but I would like to just enjoy the sun and walk along the beach." No sooner had he said this than some woman started making her way towards him. "I don't believe this," he said. "She couldn't possibly recognize me. This is an oversized robe I'm wearing and these glasses practically cover my face! She's coming right towards me. Oh no! She's going for my feet!"

The woman lunged toward Jesus' feet as though she were moving in for a tackle. There was no escape for Jesus. "Please rabbi, my daughter is all messed up inside and I need your help. Actually, 'messed up' is putting it mildly. She is having a devil of a time of it!"

As soon as the woman started talking, Jesus felt uneasy. He picked up her accent and knew immediately she was no Jew. She was Greek, and that didn't sit well with Jesus. Jews and Greeks were not friendly toward one another. "Not only has this woman cornered me when I was looking for a little privacy, but she isn't even Jewish. What have I done to deserve all this?" Then he looked down at the woman who still had her arms around his legs. "What is your name?" he asked.

The woman looked up at Jesus as if she were holding on to some trophy. "Irene."

Jesus smiled. "Irene, it's OK; you can let go. I'm not going to run away. This robe I'm wearing wouldn't permit it."

Irene slowly relaxed her grip but she wouldn't let go completely. She didn't quite seem to believe him when he said he wouldn't run away.

"Irene. I want to be honest with you, perfectly honest. What comfort I have to give, I've pretty much decided to restrict to my own people. I've got enough of their problems to handle for a lifetime." Irene just looked at Jesus as though she didn't get what he was driving at or did know what he meant and didn't buy the point he was trying to make.

"I don't think Irene is getting my point," Jesus thought as he tried to make the same point in another way. "Irene, let's put it this way. You don't take food that's meant for children and give it to the dogs." As soon as he said this, Jesus said to himself, "Now that was a dumb thing to say. These people aren't dogs. Did I say that?" He was about to tell Irene that what he said he really didn't mean. However, Irene didn't seem particularly disturbed by what he said. On the other hand, she squeezed the grip around his legs and this may have been a way of letting Jesus know just who had the power at that moment.

"Rabbi," she said with the confidence of one who knew how to get what she wanted, "even the dogs get the leftovers!"

Jesus' first reaction was, "I knew it! I should never have put the matter that way to begin with." His other reaction was in line with everything he was about in life. He said, "Irene, you're some woman! You won't take 'no' for an answer. I couldn't turn down your request if I wanted. If your daughter has been having a devil of a time, when you go home you will find that the devil has left her because no devil could hang around long with someone like you in the house."

Irene was ecstatic, so ecstatic she didn't even notice she was hauling Jesus with her as she started moving away on her knees. "Irene," Jesus said softly, "it's OK; you can let go."

"Thank you, Rabbi, thank you," Irene said as she let go of Jesus and disappeared. Jesus took off his colored glasses, looked at them, took the hood off his head, and laughed a laugh into the sun that was marvelous to behold as he said, "So much for a day off!"

Reflection: Self Discovery

There are several kinds of healing in this story, but we actually never see the one that we generally label a healing. That healing is of Irene's daughter. The more important healings in the story we might not even think to call healings. What are they?

Miriam Moskevitz's father didn't die. He just pretended so someone would notice him. Jesus takes him aside, splits a bottle of beer, and gets him interested in life by affirming his attractiveness at age ninety. That is a miracle of the first order. And it is the kind of miracle that all of us need as we grow older. If Jesus were walking the earth today, he would have his hands full just healing all the people who are in need of being affirmed because no one notices.

The other healing miracles that Jesus works are not described. Nor do they need to be described. Whatever the specific problem of each person, we know Jesus' healing includes spending time and touching people where they hurt. If it sounds a little bit like mom's old-fashioned healing method of kissing boo-boos, that's OK. The human and humane touch when the doctor visits the patient and spends time alleviating the person's fears and anxieties is very often what people desperately need. Spending time with people is not the same as wasting time, although some doctors, clergy, and other caregivers may identify the two.

There is still another healing miracle and this time it is the healing in Jesus himself. He wanted a day off and he finds himself interrupted by a woman who isn't even Jewish. His reaction is the reaction of any first-century Jew toward any non-Jew; his reaction is much the same as our reactions toward those who are different from us. It is biased and prejudiced. And no sooner do the words leave his mouth than he realizes his prejudice and how it automatically governed his denial of her request.

What are we to think of this? Jesus reacting in a biased way? He is a man of his times and consequently he absorbed, among other things, its patterns of relating to others. But Jesus transcends and moves beyond relating as a man of his times. He catches himself, and the ministry of compassion that is unique to him wins out. Jesus is healed of the narrow, confining, stereotypical way of understanding and an equally narrow way of behaving toward the Syrophoenician woman. He heals her daughter and in healing her daughter, the Word becomes more fully human.

Index

Biblical Text:

Matthew 8:1-4 73
Matthew 17:1-9 129
Mark 1:21-28 19
Mark 1:32-34 29
Mark 2:1-12 105
Mark 5:1 137
Mark 5:25-34 . . . . 81, 89
Mark 7:24-29 145
Mark 7:31-37 3
Mark 8:22-26 45
Mark 9:14-29 97
Mark 10:46-52 11
Luke 10:1-10 55
Luke 13:10-17 121
Luke 17:11-19 113
Luke 18:1-8 63
John 5:1-15 37

Cycle A:

2nd Sunday of Lent 129

Cycle B:

4th Sunday 19
5th Sunday 29
7th Sunday 105
13th Sunday 81, 89
23rd Sunday 3
30th Sunday 11

Cycle C:

14th Sunday 55
28th Sunday 113
29th Sunday 63

Feastdays:

St. Luke, October 18th 55
Thanksgiving 113
Transfiguration, August 6th (Cycle A) 129

Lent:

2nd Sunday in Lent Cycle A 129
Tuesday of the 4th Week 37

Year I:

Monday of the 30th Week 121
Wednesday of the 32nd Week 113
Saturday of the 32nd Week 63

Year I and II:

Monday of the 4th Week 97, 137
Tuesday of the 1st Week 19
Tuesday of the 4th Week 81, 89

Wednesday of the 2nd Week 29
Wednesday of the 6th Week 45
Thursday of the 5th Week 14
Thursday of the 8th Week 11
Friday of the 5th Week 3
Friday of the 12th Week 73

Stories and Parables
—— *for Ministry* ——

from Resource Publications, Inc.

WINTER DREAMS and Other Such Friendly Dragons
by Joseph J. Juknialis
Paperbound $7.95
87 pages, 6" x 9"
ISBN 0-89390-010-9
This book of 15 dramas, fairy tales and fables dances with images that spark into clarity old and treasured principles. Discover the blessings concealed in "If Not For Our Unicorns" and "In Search Of God's Tracks." Especially good for retelling is the Advent story, "Sealed With A Dream."

WHEN GOD BEGAN IN THE MIDDLE
by Joseph J. Juknialis
Paperbound $7.95
101 pages, 6" x 9"
ISBN 0-89390-027-3
Here is fantasy adventure for young and old alike. In this collection of stories, find out what lies "Twixt Spring and Autumn" and "Why Water Lost Her Color". Meet Greta and Andy, whose mountain is "Carved Out of Love."

A STILLNESS WITHOUT SHADOWS
by Joseph J. Juknialis
Paperbound $7.95
75 pages, 6" x 9"
ISBN 0-89390-081-8
This collection contains 13 new stories, including: "The Cup," "The Golden Dove," "Bread that Remembers," "Golden Apples," "Pebbles at the Wall," and "Lady of the Grand." You'll find an appendix that tells you how to use the stories in church, school, or at home.

ANGELS TO WISH BY: A Book of Story-Prayers
by Joseph J. Juknialis
Paperbound $7.95
136 pages, 6" x 9"
ISBN 0-89390-051-6
A delight to read as a collection of stories, as well as a book well suited for use in preparing liturgies and paraliturgical celebrations. Scripture references, prayers, and activities that show how these story-prayers can be put to practical use in your church situation accompany most of the stories.

NO KIDDING, GOD, WHERE ARE YOU?
Parables of Ordinary Experience
by Lou Ruoff
Paperbound $7.95
100 pages, 5½" x 8½"
ISBN 0-89390-141-5
Gifted storyteller, Fr. Ruoff, helps find God for those who sometimes feel that he is hiding. These 25 stories work as effective homilies and are great for your planning — they are accompanied by Scripture references according to each season of the liturgical year.

THE MAGIC STONE and Other Stories for the Faith Journey
by James L. Henderschedt
Paperbound $7.95
95 pages, 5½" x 8½"
ISBN 0-89390-116-4
Share the word of Scripture in the context of today's lifestyles. These stories will make you want to read them aloud to let the word come to life for your congregation, prayer group, or adult education class. Readers and listeners alike are invited to think — about the "moral" of the story, about the story's significance in their lives, and about how this story can help their spiritual growth.

THE TOPSY-TURVY KINGDOM
More Stories for Your Faith Journey
by James L. Henderschedt
Paperbound $7.95
126 pages, 5½" x 8½"
ISBN 0-89390-177-6
21 stories that turn the ordinary world upside down and inside out. Use them for preaching — they're keyed to the lectionary — or in religious education. Your listeners will see themselves in the characters Henderschedt paints so vividly — perhaps in Jason, the bully from the title story, or in the two frail young people in "The Dance."

Fresh Storytelling in Ministry Ideas!

TELLING STORIES LIKE JESUS DID: Creative Parables for Teachers
by Christelle L. Estrada
Paperbound $8.95, REVISED & EXPANDED!
100 pages, 5½" x 8½", ISBN 0-89390-097-4
Bring home the heart of Jesus' message by personalizing the parables of Luke. Each chapter includes introductory comments and questions, an easy-to-use storyline, and discussion questions for primary, secondary, and junior high grades. Newly revised.

BALLOONS! CANDY! TOYS! and Other Parables for Storytellers
by Daryl Olszewski
Paperbound $8.95
100 pages, 5½" x 8½", ISBN 0-89390-069-9
Learn how to make stories into faith experiences for children and adults. Learn to tell about "An Evening With Jesus" and "From Hostility to Hospitality." Nine delightful parables plus commentary that shows readers how to tell the stories, how to use them in preaching and teaching, and how to come up with new stories.

Stories for Children

BOOMERANG and Other Easter Stories
by Fr. Chester Wrzaszczak
Paperbound $7.95
100 pages, 5½" x 8½", ISBN 0-89390-131-8
Allow Fr.Chester's Depression-era childhood stories to entertain you ten times over. This companion volume to his *St. Francis and the Christmas Miracle* brings about a bright, new Easter outlook. These ten stories will make you understand, through a child's experience, the solemnity of Good Friday and the joy of the Resurrection.

**ST. FRANCIS AND THE CHRISTMAS MIRACLE
and Other Stories for Children**
by Fr. Chester Wrzaszczak
Paperbound $7.95
100 pages, 5½" x 8½", ISBN 0-89390-091-5
Inviting stories for adults and children written from a time when goodwill towards others, especially during Christmas, gave many a warm and renewed faith in man. Join Fr. Chester in recalling his Depression-era childhood, when money was scarce and what people lacked in money, they made up for in love and imagination.

PARABLES FOR LITTLE PEOPLE
by Lawrence Castagnola, S.J.
Paperbound $7.95
101 pages, 5½" x 8½", ISBN 0-89390-034-6
Be forewarned. When you pick up these stories, you risk being transformed. The language of children relays the message of these 16 powerful parables. Castagnola artfully reaches children in preaching, in teaching, and in the simple pleasures of storytelling.

MORE PARABLES FOR LITTLE PEOPLE
by Lawrence Castagnola, S.J.
Paperbound $7.95
100 pages, 5½" x 8½", ISBN 0-89390-095-8
Enjoy this companion volume to *Parables for Little People*. It gives you 15 imaginative children's stories with happy, positive messages. Find seven stories concerning the Gospel themes of sharing, caring, non-violence, and women's rights. Discover still other stories that retell Gospel stories—without mentioning the names of the original characters.

Stories for Growth and Change

by Andre Papineau

BREAKTHROUGH: Stories of Conversion
by Andre Papineau
Paperbound $7.95
139 pages, 5½" x 8½", ISBN 0-89390-128-8
Here is an essential resource for RCIA, Cursillo, and renewal programs. You and your group will witness what takes place inside Papineau's characters as they change. These stories will remind you that change, ultimately, is a positive experience. You'll find reflections from a psychological point of view following each section to help you to help others deal with their personal conversions keyed to the lectionary.

JESUS ON THE MEND: Healing Stories for Ordinary People
by Andre Papineau
Paperbound $7.95
150 pages, 5½" x 8½", ISBN 0-89390-140-7
You know that everybody, at some time, needs to heal or be healed. Here are 18 Gospel-based stories that illustrate four aspects of healing: Acknowledging the Need, Reaching Out for Help, The Healer's Credentials, and The Healer's Therapy. Also included are helpful reflections following each story, focusing on the process of healing that takes place. Better understand healing, so that you, like Jesus, can bring comfort to those who hurt.

BIBLICAL BLUES: Growing Through Set-Ups and Let-Downs
by Andre Papineau
Paperbound $7.95, NEW!
160 pages, 5½" x 8½", ISBN 0-89390-157-1
Be transformed while you are deep into your own personal recovery. This book of biblical stories acknowleges the way people set themselves up for a let-down to come later. Papineau consoles us in revealing that Jesus, ever the playful one, often enters the scene to puncture a balloon, a deflating event that somehow leads to spiritual growth.